Cooking with
Chiles

Inspiring | Educating | Creating | Entertaining

Brimming with creative inspiration, how-to projects, and useful information to enrich your everyday life, quarto.com is a favorite destination for those pursuing their interests and passions.

First Published in 2022 by The Harvard Common Press, an imprint of The Quarto Group,
100 Cummings Center, Suite 265-D, Beverly, MA 01915, USA.
T (978) 282-9590 F (978) 283-2742 Quarto.com

The Harvard Common Press titles are also available at discount for retail, wholesale, promotional, and bulk purchase. For details, contact the Special Sales Manager by email at specialsales@quarto.com or by mail at The Quarto Group, Attn: Special Sales Manager, 100 Cummings Center, Suite 265-D, Beverly, MA 01915, USA.

26 25 24 23 22   1 2 3 4 5

ISBN: 978-0-7603-7518-1
Content in this book was previously published in *Some Like It Hot: Savory Flavors from the World's Hot Zones* (Harvard Common Press, 2005) by Clifford A. Wright.

Digital edition published in 2022
eISBN: 978-0-7603-7519-8

Library of Congress Cataloging-in-Publication Data is available

Cover Design and Page Layout: Ashley Prine, Tandem Books
Cover Image: Richard Swearinger
Interior Photographs: Richard Swearinger
Image Credits: Shutterstock: interior decorative elements used throughout © HuHu; 7 © YARUNIV Studio; 8 © bioraven; 9 (Cubanelle) © chantel; 9 (Bell) © Nattika; 9 (Poblano) © Quang Ho; 9 (Bird's Eye) © Rak ter samer; 9 (Jalapeño) © Silvy78; 9 (serrano) © Tiger Images; 9 (Thai) © Trong Nguyen; 9 (Habanero) © XYZ images; 9 (upper right) © yarrbush; 11 © mady70

Printed in China

Always follow the most up-to-date food safety guidelines when cooking, handling, serving, and storing food, and use common sense when working with kitchen utensils and appliances. Food safety guidelines can be found at www.fsis.usda.gov.

Cooking with
Chiles

Spicy Meat, Seafood, Noodle, Rice, and Vegetable-Forward
Recipes from Around the World

Clifford A. Wright

HARVARD
COMMON
PRESS

Contents

Introduction

The World of Spice

Our eyes nearly popped out of our heads when my daughter Dyala and I saw our Chongqing Spicy Chicken arrive. The platter was covered with hundreds of red chiles. I don't think I'm exaggerating, although we didn't actually count them. We were slightly alarmed, but game. The other diners in this San Francisco restaurant were gringos, and they whispered as they rubbernecked toward our table. It was clear to us that this dish was not on the menu and that we had successfully communicated to our Chinese waitress that we might look like Americans, but our culinary souls were Sichuan. The platter sat in front of us for a while because we weren't sure whether we were supposed to attack it or cleverly dodge the chiles like a soldier ducking withering fire. We decided to eat, slowly, and with chopsticks, picking around the chiles. It was amazing! The chicken knuckles—that's what I called them—were actually a section of the wing and so tender that you could eat the delicate bones as well. The flavor was intense, very intense, and delicious, very delicious, and hot, very hot. We started sweating and continued eating, quietly, without a word to each other. We ate all of it and looked up, sniffling. Dyala said, "That was incredible, Dad. Do you really think you can re-create it?" "I must," I responded, "because I must have this again." Well, this book has Chongqing Spicy Chicken (page 94) and other amazingly hot recipes from what I call the "Hot Zone," the spiciest, hottest cuisines in the world.

No, I'm not a masochist and I'm not a chile-head. I have simply become fascinated with the cuisines around the world that are so piquant.

The "Hot" Spices

What exactly is it that gives food flavor and heat? The easy answer is spice. A spice is defined as any of a number of aromatic vegetable products used to season or flavor foods. Spices are used to change the way food tastes. The expression "spice it up" means to add spice to food to make it taste better or more interesting. Spices also seem to play a role in aiding digestion and in

The Hottest Cuisines in the World

Conventional wisdom would have you believe that the hottest cuisines are around the equator, as one culinary band circling the world, or that they are associated with very hot climates. But what makes these fiery cuisines so interesting is that many of them are culinary islands; there is no contiguous geographical belt of culinary spiciness. The hottest cuisines in the world are Peru-Bolivian, including the Amazon Basin; Mexican; southwestern United States; Louisiana Cajun; Jamaican and some other Caribbean islands; West African and a few central and southern African countries; Algerian-Tunisian; Ethiopian; Yemeni; Indo-Pakistani; Thai; Indonesian-Malay; Sichuan; and Korean.

preserving food by inhibiting bacterial growth but their most important use is making food taste better.

The flavor of spices comes from volatile oils in their chemical composition. But some spices do more than that. They also create a hot or burning sensation in the mouth. For millennia spices provided a piquancy that enlivened the taste of food, and in traditional societies there was a powerful medicinal reason for the love of spices, too. In the Old World—Europe, Africa, and Asia—black pepper, mustard, ginger, and other spices provided gastronomic heat. In the New World, a single family of plants produced fruit that was so powerfully spicy that it was used as the single piquant spice. The chile provided both the Incas in Peru and the Aztecs in Mexico with a powerful burning sensation, although the plant was being used thousands of years before the Incas and Aztecs. Once Europeans arrived in the New World and the chile plant began its diffusion throughout the world, it replaced black pepper as the hottest spice, although it did not replace any spices wholesale; it simply joined them in the pantry of the cook.

No other spice comes close to the piquancy of the New World chile, which is the source of all modern chile varieties, and so the star of this show—and the focus of this book—will be the chile. Before the discovery of the New World the spices used for piquancy in the Old World were limited to several spices that had varying degrees of "hotness." They varied not only from each other but could also vary depending on the cultivar, where they were grown, when they were harvested, how they had been aged or stored, and some other factors. These spices, which you will encounter in boxes and recipes throughout this book, are: garlic, ajwain, clove, galangal, grains of paradise, ginger, black pepper, long pepper, and mustard.

Several other spices are generally considered pungent, but not piquant or hot: Sichuan peppercorns (the only one of this category I use in these recipes), wasabi, cubeb pepper, Ashanti pepper, horseradish, horseradish tree, Negro pepper, water pepper, jungle chile, jungle pepper, and Tasmanian pepper. Finally, there is one quite pungent plant, the radish, a member of the cabbage family, which is actually never used as a spice but as a vegetable and therefore is not included in this roundup.

Just How Spicy Is Spicy?

The piquancy of chiles is measured by what are called Scoville Heat Units. Although each type of chile is associated with a certain Scoville range, it's not always reliable, as growers are growing all kinds of chile cultivars, for instance, jalapeños that are not hot. The majority of the peppers rated on the Scoville site cannot be found in a market. And the hottest ones are not even edible.

Scoville Scale

Pure Capsaicin / 15,000,000

Pepper Spray / 2,000,000 – 5,300,000

Carolina Reaper / 1,400,000 – 2,200,000

Trinidad Scorpion / 1,200,000 – 2,000,000

Ghost Pepper / 855,000 – 1,041,427

Chocolate Habanero / 425,000 – 577,000

Red Savina Habanero / 350,000 – 577,000

Fatali / 125,000 / 325,000

Habanero / 100,000 – 350,000

Scotch Bonnet / 100,000 – 350,000

Thai Pepper / 50,000 – 100,000

Cayenne Pepper / 30,000 – 50,000

Tabasco Pepper / 30,000 – 50,000

Serrano P epper / 10,000 – 23,000

Hungarian / 5,000 – 10,000

Jalapeno / 2,500 – 8,000

Pablano / 1,000 – 1,500

Anaheim / 500 – 2,500

Pepperoncini / 100 – 500

Bell Pepper / 0

Recipe HOTNESS! Scale

For the purposes of this book, I came up with the hotness scale as a way to categorize the intensity of a recipe's heat. But keep in mind that this scale is not always a reliable or consistent guide. The problem is that the piquancy of chiles is not standard; they may differ within the same bin, and certainly from market to market, and definitely from state to state. This means that making a recipe with chiles purchased in a part of the country known for spice may produce food so hot that it's inedible, while making a recipe with a hotness scale ranking of Thermonuclear using chiles from a region not known for spice may turn out to have very little heat at all. This is all to say that when you cook with chiles, it's a crap shoot; you never know what you're going to get. My best advice is to sit back and enjoy the experience. Make the surprise of the flavors and heat part of the fun.

Piquant 🌶
Incendiary 🌶 🌶
Blistering 🌶 🌶 🌶
Molten 🌶 🌶 🌶 🌶
Thermonuclear 🌶 🌶 🌶 🌶 🌶

Selecting Chiles

The recipes in this book call for a variety of specific chile cultivars, all of which have different levels of heat. I try to give alternatives, but this chart will give you an idea of what you might likely find in your market and how to concoct substitutes.

Weaponized chiles: habanero, Scotch bonnet, African bird

Extremely hot chiles: Thai, bird's eye, finger-type, *rocoto*, piquín, *chiltepin*, cayenne, Tabasco, *ají*, de árbol, cherry, cascabel

Very hot chiles: jalapeño, serrano, guajillo, Dundicutt, Kashmiri, yellow

Hot chiles: poblano/ancho, pasilla, Anaheim, California Hot, New Mexico

Not hot chiles: Cubanelle, bell

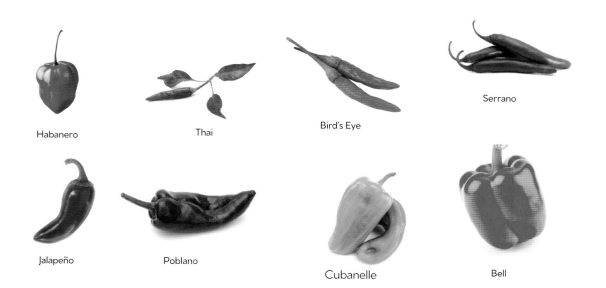

Habanero

Thai

Bird's Eye

Serrano

Jalapeño

Poblano

Cubanelle

Bell

Handling Chiles

One very important note: Handling chiles requires care and thoughtfulness. Wash your hands thoroughly afterward with plenty of soap and warm water, and *never* put your fingers near mucus membranes of your body—eyes, mouth, nose, and so on—after handling chiles. Some people's skin can be sensitive to chiles as well, so it may benefit you to wear thin disposable plastic gloves when handling chiles.

Acclimating to Extremely Hot Cuisines

This book features dishes from the most piquant cuisines in the world. Many of these foods prepared authentically will defeat the typical American palate, and when you encounter them in restaurants in the United States, rest assured you are not eating the real thing. In this book, you will meet the real thing. This doesn't mean that all of the preparations in these cuisines are piquant. Some dishes aren't. And it doesn't mean that everyone in the populations where these cuisines originated loves chiles. Some Mexicans don't care for them, for instance. But there is one thing for sure—the majority of the people from these cultures do love very hot food.

Tips on How to Build a Spice Tolerance

Remember that tolerance and appreciation for piquant foods must be built up slowly and incrementally. Therefore, if you are unfamiliar with spicy foods or want to get a better sense of the range of how hot these cuisines are, you can do one of two things. First, you can start by choosing recipes marked with this symbol 🌶 (see box), and then move up to those marked 🌶🌶, and so on. Second, you can Americanize the recipe. Americanizing means reducing the amount of chiles called for by half or three-quarters for the hottest recipes—those marked with a 🌶🌶🌶, 🌶🌶🌶🌶, or 🌶🌶🌶🌶🌶. You can desensitize yourself to the irritation of the capsaicin, and once you do, the burning sensation slowly dissipates,

Reflections on Authenticity in Cuisines

In writing this book I've thought a lot about authenticity and what that means. When I was testing the recipes I would begin first by stocking the pantry entirely with all the ingredients I might possibly need, so that I could cook a particular cuisine on a whim. This approach made both the testing and eating less of a hassle and quite pleasant, as well as shortening the learning curve. I would also stick with a particular cuisine for weeks or months, immersing myself in the culture so that I could get to the point where I could legitimately invent recipes (although only a few of these innovative recipes are in this book). With cuisines I was unfamiliar with, I would educate myself by reading, traveling, eating at the restaurants, and relying on natives of that culture.

One of my friends is Korean and a very good cook. She set up a schedule for my "Korean" education, which included shopping together in Korean markets in Koreatown in Los Angeles and cooking together. What I found so interesting, and which showed me how rigid my idea of authenticity had been, was that she took all kinds of shortcuts that make cooking easier for her without the loss of "authenticity of taste." She said that I shouldn't worry about how her grandmother did it since how she does it is just as "authentic." So, she argued, I shouldn't confuse "antique" or "old style" with "authentic." The modern way of a young Korean cook living in America is just as "authentic." What this means for the recipes in this book is that they are "modern authentic world cuisine," where each individual culture is respected. This is not fusion cuisine, but world cuisine for American cooks. It's okay for you to buy that jar of kimchi, because Korean Americans are no more likely to make kimchi at home than German Americans to make sauerkraut.

leaving an agreeable flavor and heightened awareness of the other flavors of the dish as well as a pleasant warmth. A novice wine drinker believes all wine tastes the same, and a novice chile eater feels only the heat of the chile. As with the subtleties of wine, chiles are as varied in heat as they are in taste and smell. Chiles, too, have a floral bouquet and various aromas and tastes, depending on their species, their cultivars, their stages of ripeness, and their processing (whether they are cooked, smoked, dried, left whole, or ground).

You can gradually increase your tolerance for foods made hot by the use of chiles to the point that others may consider you mad. The neophyte will claim that the heat dulls their senses—and that is true. That's why one increases tolerance slowly and gradually, for at the other end of the spectrum the foods that are very hot heighten the sense of taste and the ability to detect subtle flavors.

As a tenderfoot, or should I say "tendermouth," the first thing you encounter when you eat spicy-hot food is the flash of hotness. You will not taste anything but only feel the pain and burn on your tongue. This is why it makes sense to start slowly and build up your tolerance for hot foods. After a while, that hot flash and discomfort recedes to the background, admittedly a hot background, and the subtle tastes of the other ingredients in the dish begin to emerge. There is a freshness, a richness, a saltiness, a savory aroma, a tang, a bitterness, a sweetness, and a heightened sensitivity to the complexity of flavors. It is all seemingly enhanced by that initial jolt of heat. Relax and let your senses become acute, and you will enjoy the experience of eating like you never have before.

A Note About the Recipes and Stocking Your Pantry

The recipes in this book are authentic—very authentic. It will be challenging for you, a home cook, to stock your pantry with all the foods needed to cook from so many diverse cuisines. But it can be done, thanks to the ethnic markets that are increasingly found in all American cities, and thanks also to the Internet. It may seem like madness if a guest should look into your pantry and see jars of *dawadawa*, fermented locust bean, dried shrimps,

kochu'jang, and harissa. And the number of dried chiles and chile powders I have! Yikes!

What all this means is that to make these recipes as if you were cooking in another country you will have to make a definite effort—although not a hard one—to find these ingredients. If you live in a city with ethnic markets, all the better. But with online shopping, the world arrives at our door. I've made a rather large effort to identify reliable online sources, so I hope you give some of them a try. There is an enormous satisfaction in contacting the little West African market in Buffalo, New York, and having your red palm oil show up two weeks later. But I recognize that not everyone is going to make this effort, so I've written the recipes to suggest alternatives or substitutes for hard-to-find items. Remember, though, that some of these substitutes are not at all like the real thing. Many of these ingredients can be found in your local supermarket, believe it or not. So if you're having trouble finding something, just ask.

Luckily, you will not need to buy new equipment. Your existing kitchenware will be more than satisfactory. One thing you might have to buy, if you don't already have it, is a wok. Otherwise, plunge in, impress your friends and family, and enjoy yourself.

Chapter 1

SOUPED-UP
Soups & Salads

Cream of Avocado Soup

3 large ripe avocados, peeled, seeded, and diced

1½ cups heavy cream

¼ cup dry sherry

1 tablespoon fresh lime juice

1 tablespoon pureed or grated onions

2 garlic cloves, ground in a mortar with 1 teaspoon salt until mushy

1 teaspoon freshly ground dried ancho chile or ½ teaspoon chile powder

1 to 3 teaspoons salt

1 teaspoon freshly ground white pepper

6 cups chicken broth (homemade or store-bought)

3 corn tortillas, quartered and fried in oil until crisp

Fresh cilantro leaves, for garnish

Makes 8 servings

This *sopa de aguacate* is from Atlixco, an area of Mexico where many avocados grow. It's creamy smooth, very flavorful, and not too hot; a nice dish to serve before chicken, pork, or salmon. For a spicier soup, you can add a small, finely chopped habanero chile. Some Mexicans eat this soup cold, like a gazpacho, but I think it's much better hot.

1. Place the avocados in a blender with the cream, sherry, lime juice, onion, and garlic and blend at high speed for 30 seconds. Season with the ancho chile, 1 teaspoon salt, and the white pepper.

2. Bring the chicken broth to a boil in a large saucepan over high heat. Reduce the heat to low and, once the broth is just simmering, add the avocado puree. Whisk the soup until smooth, taste, and add the remaining 2 teaspoons salt if desired. Serve hot, garnished with the tortilla pieces and cilantro.

Korean Clam Soup

Makes 2 to 4 servings

This simple dish is called *jo gae gook* in Korean. It is beautiful to look at and its tastes are hot and straightforward. This is a recipe I would recommend to someone who has never made Korean food, because it's very easy and tastes very Korean and will be as good as anything you could order in a Korean restaurant.

Pour the water into a pot with the clams. Bring to a boil, then reduce the heat to medium. Just after the clams open up, after 4 to 8 minutes, take them out with a slotted spoon. Discard any clams that remain firmly shut. Add the salt, ground chile, tofu, and scallion to the broth and cook for another minute. Put the clams back in the pot and heat for 1 minute. Serve garnished with the fresh chopped chile.

1 quart water

10 small littleneck or Manila clams, cleaned

2 teaspoons salt

1½ teaspoons ground Korean red chile or 1 teaspoon ground red chile

3 ounces firm tofu, diced

1 scallion, white and green parts, cut on the bias in ¼-inch slices

1 fresh red jalapeño chile, chopped

Korean Red Chile

This flaky dried red chile powder is ubiquitous in Korean cooking, and it can be bought in Korean markets and online. But this chile mixture, which is bright red and mildly hot, is so similar to a particular kind of Mexican chili powder that you might be able to get away with this substitution. The one I'm thinking of is made with equal parts dried ground pasilla chile, New Mexico Hot (a kind of Anaheim chile), and California chile (another kind of Anaheim chile), and should say so on the label ingredients.

Shrimp Soup
from Rinconada

Makes 4 servings

This recipe, called *sopa de camaron rinconada,* is adapted from Patricia Quintana's *The Taste of Mexico* (Stewart, Tabori & Chang, 1986). Rinconada is a small village between Veracruz and Xalapa, and this soup is sold at food stands there as a breakfast soup. It's downright ambrosial and is great with warmed-up corn tortillas. The epazote called for may be hard to find; fresh cilantro may be used instead, but it's not needed as this soup is incredible without it. I usually serve this for dinner with corn tortillas and beer.

1. Place the shrimp heads, if using, and the shrimp shells in a large saucepan and cover with the water. Bring to a boil, then reduce the heat to low, and simmer for 1 hour. Strain and save the broth, discarding the shells and heads.

2. In a large saucepan, heat the olive oil over medium-high heat. Cook the onions, stirring, until soft and slightly golden, about 8 minutes. Add the tomatoes, reduce the heat to medium, and cook slowly, stirring occasionally, until the liquid from the tomatoes is mostly evaporated, 18 to 20 minutes. Add the chiles and shrimp broth and bring to a boil over high heat. Season with salt.

3. Add the shrimp and epazote, if using. Reduce the heat slightly and cook uncovered, with the soup barely bubbling, until the shrimp are orange-red and firm, 10 to 12 minutes. Reduce the heat more if the soup is bubbling too much. Serve with a wedge of lime.

3 pounds fresh shrimp with heads left on several shrimp, the remainder removed and saved, shells removed and saved, or 1½ pounds headless shrimp, shells removed and saved

2 quarts water

⅓ cup extra-virgin olive oil

2 medium-size white onions, cut in half and thinly sliced

3 large tomatoes, cut in half, seeds squeezed out, and grated against the largest holes of a grater

2 large fresh green jalapeño chiles, sliced

Salt to taste

2 leafy sprigs epazote (see below) or fresh cilantro (optional)

1 lime, quartered

Epazote

This musty herb, reminiscent of a combination of sage and parsley, is used in Mexican cuisine and can be found in farmers markets in the western United States. The leaves of epazote were originally used to season soups and stews made by the Chinatec and Mazatec and other tribes in Mexico. As it can be hard to find, I recommend that you just consider it optional.

Fish Soup Piquant

6 large garlic cloves, peeled

2 teaspoons cumin seeds

½ teaspoon salt, plus more to your taste

½ cup extra-virgin olive oil

1 medium-size onion, chopped

1 tablespoon tomato paste

8½ cups water

1 tablespoon hot paprika

1 teaspoon cayenne pepper

½ teaspoon Harissa (page 25)

½ teaspoon freshly ground black pepper

2 fresh green finger-type chiles or 3 fresh green jalapeño chiles, stemmed and seeded

2 celery ribs, chopped

3 carrots, sliced

Pinch of saffron threads, crumbled

10 sprigs parsley, tied in cheesecloth

1 bay leaf

1½ to 3 pounds mixed fish fillets

1 lemon, quartered, or 1 Preserved Lemon (page 40), quartered

Makes 4 servings

This is a fish soup or stew, *maraqat al-hut*, made in the Mediterranean seaport of Sfax in Tunisia. It is traditional for the feast of the breaking of the Ramadan fast. The most common and popular fish at the Sfax fish market are grouper, usually chosen for this stew, and scorpionfish, annular bream, hake, and red gurnard. Whatever fish you choose ideally should be local and fresh. Choose two from the following suggestions: grouper, porgy (scup), red snapper, redfish (ocean perch), ocean pout, cod, haddock, wolffish (ocean catfish), and hake. Of course, if your fish store doesn't have these, then ask the fishmonger to recommend two that are medium to firm fleshed. The broth can be eaten separately from the fish with grilled, toasted, or fried bread or with macaroni cooked in the broth. Or the diners can serve themselves a piece of fish to put in the soup bowl with the broth.

1. In a mortar, pound the garlic, cumin seeds, and ½ teaspoon salt until you have a paste. Set aside.

2. In a large stockpot or casserole, heat the olive oil over high heat and cook the onion, stirring, until softened, 1 to 2 minutes.

3. Meanwhile, dissolve the tomato paste in ½ cup of the water and add to the stockpot along with the paprika, cayenne pepper, harissa, black pepper, and garlic paste. Add 4 cups of the water and cook on high heat for 10 minutes.

4. Add the remaining 4 cups water, the chiles, celery, carrots, saffron, parsley, and bay leaf and season with salt. Reduce the heat to medium-low and simmer for 30 minutes. Strain the broth through a fine-mesh strainer, discarding the vegetables. Return the broth to the stockpot.

5. Bring the broth to a furious boil over high heat. Add the fish and cook for 15 minutes. Remove the fish from the stockpot. Serve the broth as a first-course soup and the fish separately as a second course with the lemon quarters, keeping it warm in a low oven.

Makes 4 servings

This refreshing yet rich northern Thai soup is called *tom kha gai*. It is quite easy to prepare and much of the flavor comes from the garnish that is stirred with the soup after it is cooked: the fresh lime juice, the chiles, the cilantro, and the *nam prik pao*, a roasted chile curry paste that can be found in most supermarkets under the name Thai red curry paste although it bears little resemblance to the actual Thai nam prik found in Thailand (for a homemade version, turn the page).

1. In a wok or large saucepan, combine 1 cup of the coconut milk with the galangal, lemongrass, and lime leaves and bring to a boil. Add the chicken, fish sauce, and sugar, reduce the heat to medium, and simmer until the chicken is white and firm, about 4 minutes. Add the remaining 1 cup coconut milk and heat to just below boiling, about 3 minutes.

2. Divide the lime juice and curry paste into individual serving bowls and ladle the soup over them. Garnish each bowl with the cilantro and crushed chiles. Serve immediately.

2 cups coconut milk (see below)

6 thin slices fresh galangal or 4 slices ginger

2 lemongrass stalks, tender parts only, chopped and crushed in a mortar

5 fresh makrut lime leaves, torn in half, or 1 tablespoon grated lime zest

¾ pound boneless, skinless chicken breast, thinly sliced

5 tablespoons Thai fish sauce

2 tablespoons palm sugar or granulated sugar

½ cup fresh lime juice

1 teaspoon Red Curry Paste (page 22)

¼ cup coarsely chopped fresh cilantro leaves

25 fresh green bird's eye chiles or 15 fresh green Thai chiles or 8 fresh green serrano chiles, crushed in a mortar

Coconut Milk and Coconut Cream

Coconut cream, or thick coconut milk, refers to the liquid left over from the first pressing of grated or shredded coconut that has steeped in boiling water. When this thick coconut milk is refrigerated, a very thick liquid, almost a solid, rises to the top, and this is called coconut cream. Coconut milk, or thin coconut milk, is the liquid left over after repeated pressings of the same coconut gratings with more boiling water. Although it is best to make these varieties of coconut milk with freshly shredded coconut, you can also use dried unsweetened shredded coconut. Supermarkets sell canned coconut milk, which can also be used. Look for organic versions to avoid preservatives and additives.

Red Curry Paste

2 teaspoons coriander seeds

2 teaspoons cumin seeds

Seeds from 3 cardamom pods

2 shallots, chopped

10 garlic cloves, peeled

15 dried chiles de árbol, soaked in tepid water for 30 minutes and drained

10 fresh red Thai chiles or 6 fresh red serrano chiles, stemmed

One 1-inch cube fresh ginger or galangal, peeled

1 tablespoon shrimp paste

1 large lemongrass stalk, tough outer portions removed, tender portions chopped

1 tablespoon green peppercorns

1 tablespoon grated makrut lime zest or regular lime zest

1 tablespoon peanut oil

2 tablespoons water

½ cup chopped fresh cilantro roots and/or stems

¼ cup loosely packed fresh basil leaves

1 teaspoon salt

½ teaspoon ground nutmeg

¼ teaspoon ground mace

Makes about 1 cup

Nam prik, or *nam prik kaeng ped daeng*, meaning spicy red curry paste, goes into many Thai curry, but it is also often served alone in Thailand. Placed in the center of the table, it is offered as a dip for raw or parboiled vegetables, using only a tiny amount since the taste is powerful. This paste is used by all segments of Thai society. It is an ancient preparation, and records indicate that it was probably eaten in the twelfth and thirteenth centuries during the Sukhothai period. At that time it was likely that *prik* was made from peppercorns. There are hundreds of versions of *nam prik*. The common flavor elements are saltiness from fish sauce, soy sauce, salt, or anchovies; sour from lime juice or tamarind; spicy from chiles; sweet from palm sugar; and aromatic from chile leaf, coconut cream, cilantro roots, garlic, shallots, or fresh turmeric, all bound with fermented fish or shrimp paste. Other ingredients can find their way in, such as pineapple, raw eggplant, or roasted mushrooms. Thai red curry paste can be found in jars in the international/Asian section of supermarkets, but I encourage you to try making your own.

1. Dry-roast the coriander, cumin, and cardamom in a small cast-iron skillet over medium-high heat without any fat for 2 minutes, or until fragrant, shaking the pan. Cool and transfer to a spice mill or a mortar and finely grind.

2. Place the toasted spices in a food processor with the shallots, garlic, dried and fresh chiles, ginger, shrimp paste, lemongrass, green peppercorns, lime zest, peanut oil, water, cilantro, basil, salt, nutmeg, and mace and run the processor until the mixture is completely smooth, 5 to 8 minutes of continuous processing. Scrape the paste into a jar with a tight-fitting lid and store in the refrigerator for up to 1 month.

Salad of Pureed Red Bell Pepper and Chile

Makes 4 servings

This Tunisian *turshy* of red bell pepper and chiles is quite different than the Levantine one of the same name, which is basically pickled turnip slices. Traditionally eaten with pieces of warmed Arabic flatbread, this can be served as a meze, salad, or side dish with grilled foods. To roast the bell peppers, arrange them in a baking dish and place in a 425°F oven until blistered black, about 35 minutes, turning to make sure all sides blacken or, for a quicker result, place in a perforated pan and roast over your cooktop's burner, about 12 minutes.

Place the bell peppers, chiles, and garlic in a food processor and blend until thoroughly pureed. Transfer to a strainer and let drain for 10 minutes. Transfer to a bowl and stir in the coriander, lemon juice, and salt. Taste and add more salt if desired. Serve at room temperature with the flatbread.

1½ pounds red bell peppers (about 6), roasted, skins removed (see headnote for instructions), cored, seeded, and chopped

3 fresh red finger-type chiles or 5 fresh red jalapeño chiles, stemmed, seeded, and chopped

6 large garlic cloves

1 tablespoon ground coriander

Juice of 1 lemon

1½ teaspoons salt, or more to your taste

Arabic flatbread or pita, warmed, for serving

Chickpea Cumin Velouté

3 cups canned chickpeas, drained

1 garlic clove, crushed

¼ cup extra-virgin olive oil

1 teaspoon ground cumin

1 teaspoon hot paprika

1 teaspoon Harissa (opposite)

1 tablespoon tomato paste

Salt and freshly ground black
    pepper to taste

1 quart water

Makes 4 servings

This simple soup, said to be a favorite of Algerian dockworkers, is healthy, filling, and has a nice spicy flavor. When I first had it, made for me years ago by an Algerian friend, I just couldn't associate it with the Algerian food with which I was already familiar. Partly this was because of the fact that it was a velouté, a French concept. My friend told me that the French had indeed heavily influenced the cuisine of Algeria, but more in terms of method and technique than in flavor, and that this soup was a good example of that. This soup can be eaten with the chickpeas either left whole or creamy as in this recipe, the way I like it.

1. In a medium saucepan, cover the chickpeas with water by an inch and bring to a boil, then reduce the heat to medium-low and cook 1 hour to make them more tender. Drain, remove as much of their white skins as possible, and set aside.

2. Put the garlic, olive oil, cumin, paprika, harissa, tomato paste, salt, and black pepper in a large saucepan or stockpot. Turn the heat to medium and sauté, stirring occasionally, for 5 minutes. Pour in the water and bring to a boil. Add the chickpeas and cook for 15 minutes.

3. Remove the chickpeas with a skimmer and puree them in a food processor until smooth. Return the chickpea puree to the soup and stir to blend. Heat for a few minutes and serve immediately.

Harissa

Makes 1 cup

Harissa is the most important prepared condiment used in Tunisian and Algerian cooking. In fact, you really need to make this recipe and keep it in the refrigerator before attempting any other Tunisian or Algerian recipe. This famous hot chile paste is also used, to a much lesser extent, in the cooking of Morocco, Libya, and even western Sicily, where they use it in fish couscous. Harissa is sold in tubes by both Tunisian and French firms, but neither can compare to your own freshly made version. To turn the harissa into a sauce for grilled meats, stir together 2 teaspoons harissa, 3 tablespoons olive oil, 2 tablespoons water, and 1 tablespoon finely chopped fresh parsley leaves.

1. Soak the chiles in tepid water to cover until soft, about 1 hour. Drain and remove the stems and seeds. Place in a food processor with the garlic, water, and olive oil. Process until a puree forms, stopping occasionally to scrape down the sides.

2. Transfer to a mixing bowl and stir in the caraway, coriander, and salt. Store in a jar and top off with olive oil, covering the surface of the paste. The harissa must always be covered with olive oil to prevent spoilage, so whenever you use some, always make sure to top it off with a little olive oil. Properly stored in the refrigerator, it will keep for 6 months to 1 year.

¼ pound dried guajillo chiles

1 ounce dried chiles de árbol

5 large garlic cloves, peeled

2 tablespoons water

2 tablespoons extra-virgin olive oil

½ teaspoon ground caraway seeds

¼ teaspoon ground coriander

1½ teaspoons salt

Extra-virgin olive oil, for topping off

Crispy Fish Salad

with Mango

½ pound firm white-fleshed fish fillet, such as catfish

Salt to taste

2 cups vegetable oil, for frying

1 shallot, thinly sliced

1 celery rib, cut into 1-inch lengths and julienned

2 tablespoons roasted peanuts, coarsely crushed

½ small, very firm green mango, julienned or shredded

2 tablespoons fresh lime juice

1 tablespoon Thai fish sauce

1 teaspoon sugar

6 large fresh mint leaves, coarsely chopped

2 tablespoons coarsely chopped fresh cilantro leaves

1 teaspoon fresh bird's eye chiles, whole, or 12 fresh green Thai chiles, thinly sliced, or 5 fresh green serrano chiles, thinly sliced

Makes 4 serving

This Thai fish salad, called *yam pla dook fu*, is a real winner that everyone likes. Maybe it's because of the two-step cooking of the fish that makes it crispy. Or maybe people just love the addition of mango and peanuts. In any case, it is a refreshing salad. Fresh bird's eye chiles may be sold under the name piquín chiles in large supermarkets and Latin markets, particularly in the Southwest. In Thailand, bird's eye chiles are known as *prik kee nu* or "mouse-dropping chiles" and Thai chiles are known as *prik kee fa* or "sky-pointing chiles."

1. Preheat the oven to 400°F. Pat the fish dry with a paper towel. Season with salt and place on a rack in a roasting pan. Bake until cooked through, 15 minutes. Remove from the oven and cool. Place the fish in a food processor with a pinch of salt and blend until finely shredded but not pureed.

2. In a wok, heat the oil until very hot and almost smoking. Add ½ cup of the fish and cook until it puffs up and turns golden brown, 1 to 2 minutes. Turn carefully and cook the other side until golden brown, 1 to 2 minutes. Remove and set aside while you continue to cook the remaining fish in approximately ½ cup portions.

3. In a bowl, break the fried fish patties into pieces. Toss gently and carefully with the shallot, celery, peanuts, mango, lime juice, fish sauce, sugar, mint, cilantro, chiles, and salt to taste. Arrange on a serving platter and let sit 15 minutes. Serve cool or at room temperature.

Daikon Salad

Makes 4 to 6 servings

This very refreshing Korean salad, from my friend Unjoo Lee Byars, is called *moo-oo-sanchae*. It is served cold as an appetizer, side dish, or salad, and is especially good in the summer with grilled foods. *Moo* is the Korean word for white radish, known as daikon in Japanese. The salad is best made a few hours before you want to eat it so that the radish can become softer and more palatable

In a medium bowl, combine the radish, cucumbers, garlic, vinegar, sesame oil, ground chile, sugar, salt, soy sauce, and oysters with their liquid, if using. Toss the ingredients together until they are well mixed. Let marinate in the refrigerator for 2 hours before serving. Serve at room temperature or slightly cool.

¾ pound white radish (daikon), peeled and julienned into 2 x ¼-inch strips

2 Persian cucumbers, peel left on and julienned into 2 x ¼-inch strips, or 1 small regular cucumber, peeled, seeded, and julienned into 2 x ¼-inch strips

2 small garlic cloves, finely chopped

5 tablespoons barley vinegar or apple cider vinegar

3 tablespoons sesame oil

3 tablespoons ground Korean red chile or 2 tablespoons ground red chile

2 tablespoons sugar

1 tablespoon salt, or more to your taste

1 teaspoon soy sauce

6 oysters (optional), freshly shucked and cut in half, with their liquid

Red Kidney Bean and Quinoa Salad

1 cup (about ½ pound) dried red kidney beans

Salt

1 tablespoon red wine vinegar

½ teaspoon freshly ground black pepper

1 cup fresh corn kernels

¾ cup (about 6 ounces) quinoa

½ cup chopped red bell pepper

½ cup chopped fresh yellow chiles (ají amarillo) or fresh yellow güero chiles or 2 teaspoons very finely chopped fresh habanero chile, seeded

¼ cup finely chopped fresh cilantro leaves

3 tablespoons finely chopped celery

⅓ cup extra-virgin olive oil

¼ cup fresh lemon juice

1 teaspoon ground cumin

Makes 4 servings

This Peruvian salad, called *ensalada de quinua y frejoles rojos*, uses the famous plant of the Incas, quinoa (*Chenopodium quinoa*). The seeds of this annual herb, native to Andean Peru and Bolivia, can be made into bread or cooked as a grain as in this dish. It is a member of the goosefoot family, as is spinach, and its leaves are often used in the same way as spinach. Quinoa (pronounced KEEN-wa) is also used in the making of the local chicha beer. This salad makes a nice accompaniment to many dishes and is also excellent as an appetizer.

1. Place the kidney beans in a medium saucepan and cover with water by several inches. Bring to a boil, salt well, then cook until tender, about 1¼ hours. Drain and transfer to a large bowl and toss with the vinegar, 1 teaspoon salt, and the black pepper while still hot.

2. Bring another medium saucepan of water to a boil and cook the corn until tender, 2 to 3 minutes. Drain, toss with the beans, and set aside to cool.

3. Place the quinoa in a strainer and rinse it well. Bring a medium saucepan of salted water to a boil, then cook the quinoa for 10 minutes. Drain through a strainer and rinse. Place the strainer over a saucepan of boiling water, making sure the quinoa doesn't touch the water. Cover the quinoa with a kitchen towel, place a large lid over the towel, and steam for 10 minutes, until tender. Remove from the saucepan and let it cool.

4. Transfer the quinoa to the bowl with the beans and corn and toss with the red bell pepper, chiles, cilantro, celery, olive oil, lemon juice, and cumin. Taste and add more salt if desired. Serve at room temperature.

Water Spinach

Water spinach (*Ipomoea aquatica* Forsk), also known as *kangkung*, is a tropical perennial water plant with delicious edible green leaves that are highly prized in the Chinese cooking of Malaysia and elsewhere in Southeast Asia. Although it is related to the American sweet potato, the roots are not eaten that often. The leaves are used in soups, curries, and stir-fries and are eaten boiled and steamed, too. The youngest leaves and shoots are eaten in salads. The only place it grows well in the United States is Florida, where it is considered a weed, although some farmers might begin cultivating it for farmers markets. Regular spinach can be substituted for it.

Gado Gado

Makes 6 servings

This recipe for tossed vegetable salad with chile peanut sauce is from Malay cuisine, but it is very popular in Indonesia, too, where the sauce is known as *saus kacang*. This recipe is adapted from Dato' Tunku Mukminah Jiwa and the Malay kitchen of the Federal Hotel in Kuala Lumpur. You may be very tempted to use peanut butter instead of the whole peanuts I call for, but think "peanuts turned into sauce" rather than something coming from a jar. It is better and no more work. Remember that skinned, roasted, and unsalted peanuts are easily found in supermarkets.

1. To make the peanut sauce, in a medium bowl, steep the tamarind paste in the water until needed.

2. In a wok, heat the vegetable oil over medium-high heat, then cook the shallots and dried and fresh chiles, stirring and tossing frequently, until the shallots are golden, about 4 minutes. Remove and place in a blender with the peanuts and blend for a few seconds.

3. Place the tamarind and its water in the blender and puree until smooth. Put the contents of the blender back into the wok along with the lime leaves, sugar, soy sauce, and salt. Bring to a boil. Continue boiling until the sauce is thick and syrupy, adding a little water if necessary to keep it fluid, 2 to 3 minutes. Taste and add more sugar and salt if desired. Let the mixture cool in the wok and set aside until it is needed.

4. To prepare the vegetables, bring a large saucepan of water to a boil and boil each vegetable in succession, removing each with a skimmer as it finishes cooking: yard-long beans for 4 minutes, bean sprouts for 1 minute, cabbage for 4 minutes, and spinach for 30 seconds. Make sure you don't overcook any of the vegetables. Assemble the vegetables on a serving plate or platter. Top with the peanut sauce and serve.

For the Peanut Sauce

1 tablespoon tamarind paste

2 cups warm water

1 tablespoon vegetable oil

3 shallots, chopped

8 dried chiles de árbol, broken in half and soaked in water until needed, drained

2 fresh red jalapeño chiles, quartered

1 cup roasted, skinned, and unsalted peanuts or ½ cup peanut butter

2 makrut lime leaves, crumbled, or ½ teaspoon grated lime zest

1 tablespoon palm sugar or brown sugar, or more to your taste

1 teaspoon soy sauce

1 teaspoon salt, or more to your taste

For the Vegetables

¼ pound yard-long beans (asparagus beans) or thin green beans, trimmed and cut into 2-inch pieces

¼ pound bean sprouts

¼ pound green cabbage, cored and chopped, or kale, thick stems removed and chopped

¼ pound water spinach or spinach, thick stems removed and chopped

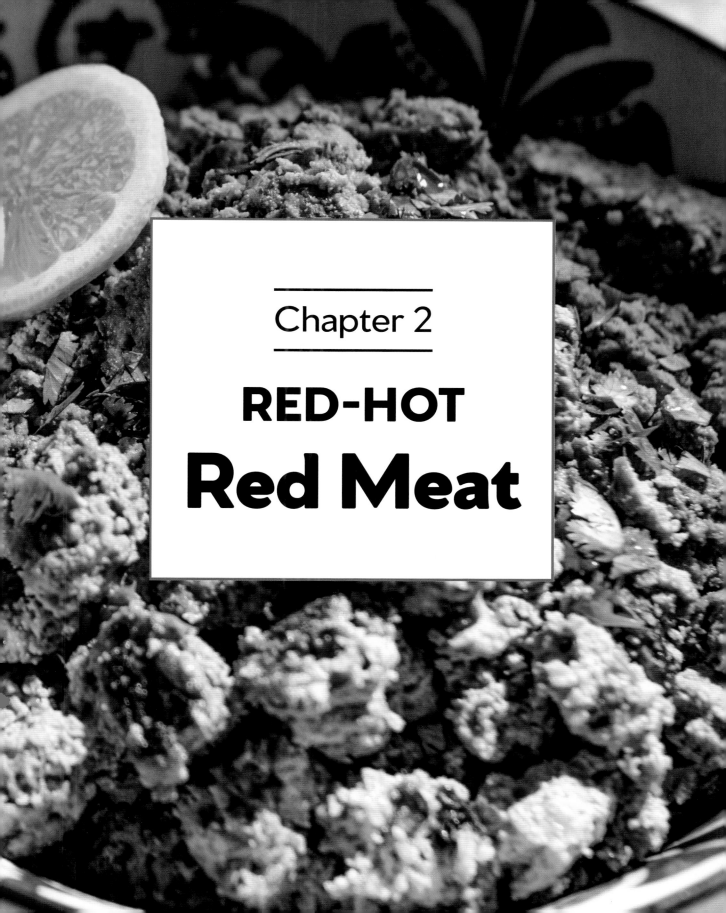

Chapter 2

RED-HOT
Red Meat

Ranchero Steaks
with Chipotle Chile Sauce

¾ pound tomatillos, husked and washed

2 large garlic cloves, peeled

3 canned chipotle chiles in adobo

2 tablespoons water

½ teaspoon salt

Freshly ground black pepper to taste

Vegetable oil, for frying

1½ pounds thin beefsteaks (see headnote), cut into 8 pieces and pounded ⅛ inch thin

Makes 4 to 6 servings

The country-style steaks called *ranchero* steaks are typical of Sonoran cooking. Thin beefsteaks are cut from the top loin, though one could also use the more expensive skirt steak, or flap steak. Mexican butchers will sell *ranchero* steaks that are pounded very thin and used for pan-frying. In order to properly brown the steaks, don't crowd them in the pan; cook them in batches. These steaks are nice served with warm flour tortillas.

1. Preheat the oven to 450°F. Arrange the tomatillos and garlic on a baking sheet and roast until the skin blackens, 20 to 25 minutes. Remove from the oven and place the tomatillos and garlic in a blender with the chipotles, water, salt, and black pepper. Blend until very smooth.

2. Meanwhile, rub a large cast-iron skillet with just a film of vegetable oil. Preheat it over high heat for 10 minutes, then cook the steaks one at a time until crispy brown on both sides, about 3 minutes in all. Remove and set aside, keeping them warm as you cook the remainder. Serve the steaks with a thin layer of chipotle chile sauce spooned over them and the remaining sauce served on the side.

Fiery Beef Shank

Makes 6 servings

This Yemeni stew is called *hur'iy*, an Arabic word that means "stewed very well until the meat shreds." And this is exactly what you do. Typically the dish is made with beef foreshank, although oxtail could be used, too. At the end of the cooking there should be just a little syrupy liquid left. An otherwise tough cut of meat is simmered with a delectable blend of spices and the resulting stew is complex, interesting, and savory. Yemen sits on the southwestern corner of the Arabian Peninsula and has been a transit point for the spice trade for two thousand years. Some of those spices clearly fell into a local pot. Serve this with rice and flatbread.

1. Put the shank in a large casserole with barely enough water to cover. Bring slowly to a boil over medium heat, skimming the foam off the surface.

2. Once the water is boiling, add the onions, garlic, tomatoes, black pepper, chiles, caraway, turmeric, saffron, cardamom, and salt. Cover, reduce the heat to low, and simmer until the meat is so tender that it shreds with the gentle tug of a fork, about 5 hours. There should be very little liquid left, but if there is, remove all the contents of the casserole with a slotted spoon, bring the broth to a boil, and boil until only 2 or 3 cups of broth remain. Return everything to the casserole and, once heated, serve immediately.

3 pounds beef shank, cut into 1-inch slices

2 large onions, cut into eighths

12 large garlic cloves, peeled and crushed

3 large tomatoes (about 1½ pounds), peeled, seeded, and quartered

2 teaspoons freshly ground black pepper

4 dried chiles de árbol, broken in half

1 teaspoon freshly ground caraway seeds

1 teaspoon ground turmeric

¼ teaspoon saffron threads, crumbled

¼ teaspoon ground cardamom

2 teaspoons salt

Chanducata

Makes 4 servings

This simple family-style summertime preparation is a recipe from the Mexican state of Michoacan. One glance and you can see why it is popular—it is quick and easy and has great flavor. It's hot, too! This dish can be eaten on a tostada (a crispy tortilla) or wrapped in a warm, soft flour tortilla.

1. In a large skillet, heat the olive oil over medium-high heat, then cook the meat with the onion, garlic, and salt, stirring occasionally, until it has browned, about 10 minutes.

2. Add the corn, tomatoes, chiles, cilantro, and mint, and then cook, stirring, until any liquid has evaporated, about 25 minutes. At the end of the cooking, if the food is sticking to the skillet, add ¼ cup water, scraping and mixing it up. Serve immediately.

2 tablespoons extra-virgin olive oil

1 pound ground beef

1 medium-size onion, chopped

4 large garlic cloves, finely chopped

Salt to taste

2 cups fresh corn kernels (about 2 cobs)

4 ripe tomatoes (about 1½ pounds), peeled and chopped

4 fresh green serrano chiles, finely chopped

¼ cup finely chopped fresh cilantro leaves

1 sprig mint, leaves only, chopped

¼ cup water, if needed

Spicy Beef
with Orange Flavor

¾ pound beef skirt steak, flank steak, or tri-tip sirloin, cut into 1½ x 1½ x ¹⁄₁₆-inch slices

¾ teaspoon salt

2½ cups peanut oil, for frying

½ cup halved and seeded dried chiles de árbol

1 tablespoon dried grated orange peel (see box to make your own)

1 teaspoon ground star anise

½ teaspoon ground Sichuan peppercorns

½ cup beef broth

1½ teaspoons fermented glutinous rice wine or rice wine (mirin) or sherry

2 teaspoons sugar

1 teaspoon Chinese black vinegar or white vinegar

½ teaspoon sesame oil

Makes 2 to 3 servings

The best cuts to use for this fast-cooking dish are tri-tip sirloin, skirt steak, flank steak, and even meat sold as *carne asada* in supermarkets in the western United States. Sichuan cooks use a fermented glutinous rice wine as part of their seasoning of this dish. Fermented rice wine consists of cooked glutinous rice sealed in a jar with wine yeast balls (sold in Chinese markets), which ferments for a few days in a warm place. It is traditionally made at home or can be purchased in Chinese markets or online. You can substitute rice wine or sherry, which work well for this dish although the flavor is different. The Chinese black vinegar (Chinkiang vinegar) is available in Chinese markets or via the Internet. Serve this dish with steamed rice if desired.

1. In a medium bowl, toss the beef with   teaspoon salt and leave for 20 minutes at room temperature.

2. In a wok, heat the peanut oil over medium-high heat until about 375°F. Cook the beef for 30 seconds, being careful as it will splatter, then remove it with a skimmer and drain.

3. Remove all but 2 tablespoons of oil from the wok. Let the remaining oil heat again over high heat, then stir-fry the chiles, orange peel, star anise, and Sichuan pepper until sizzling and fragrant, about 15 seconds, keeping your head away from the fumes of the chiles. Add the cooked beef, beef broth, rice wine, sugar, and the remaining ½ teaspoon salt and stir-fry until the liquid is nearly absorbed, about 4 minutes. When most of the liquid has evaporated, add the vinegar and sesame oil and stir. Serve immediately.

Dried Orange Peel

The dried orange peel used in the recipe is readily found in jars in the spice section of supermarkets, but I prefer making my own. Using the largest holes of a four-sided grater, grate 1 large orange, place the peel in a baking dish, and bake in a 250°F oven for 15 minutes, then turn the heat off and leave for another 15 minutes. The fragrance of the dried orange is remarkable, and you will be tempted to use it in your general cooking.

Beef Stew
with Chiles, Cassava, and Plantains

Makes 8 servings

This hearty one-pot meal is called *ebbeh* and is quite filling with all the root vegetables. *Ebbeh* or *eba* can mean either cassava flour pudding or a kind of African yam. The African yam is not the same thing as the American sweet potato, which is sometimes called a yam. It is a very large, bland root vegetable and is barely sweet. Its closest relative would be the malanga or *ñame* sold in supermarkets serving Caribbean and Latin American populations. Many supermarkets actually carry this item, usually tucked away with their more exotic items. But if you can't find it, it is better to use potato than American yam. And when shopping for ripe plantains, look for those with skin that is mottled black or brown. The proportion of meat to vegetables in this recipe is in line with what would be typical in West Africa. Cassava must always be cooked as consuming it raw is toxic.

1. Place the meat in a Dutch oven and cover with water. Bring to a boil, then reduce the heat to medium and simmer briskly for 20 minutes, skimming the foam off.

2. Place the tomatoes, onion, and chiles in a blender and blend until smooth. Add to the pot, along with the cubed cassava, yam, plantains, peanut oil, and salt. Continue cooking over medium heat until the vegetables are very tender, about 3 hours, adding cupfuls of water every time the stew gets very thick. You'll probably use 6 to 8 cups of water.

3. Once the root vegetables and plantains are tender, mash some of the vegetable pieces against the side of the pot to thicken the stew. Add the fish to the pot, reduce the heat to low, and continue cooking at a simmer until heated through, well blended, and thick, about 15 minutes. Serve immediately.

½ pound beef stew meat, cut into 1-inch cubes

¾ pound ripe tomatoes, peeled, halved, and seeded

1 large onion, cut into eighths

10 fresh green jalapeño chiles, stemmed

1 pound cassava root, peeled and cut into 1-inch cubes

1 pound African yam, malanga, ñame, or boiling potatoes, peeled and cut into 1-inch cubes

1 pound ripe plantains or taro, peeled and cut into 1-inch cubes

½ cup peanut oil

2 teaspoons salt

½ pound smoked fish, such as herring, haddock, trout, or albacore, skin and bones removed

Braised Beef

with Capers and Preserved Lemon

2 tablespoons extra-virgin
olive oil

1 pound beef tri-tip sirloin, cut
into ½-inch cubes

½ pound beef bone, with marrow
and some meat on it or a beef
shank steak

1 large onion, chopped

1 tablespoon cayenne pepper, or
to taste

1 teaspoon ground coriander

2 teaspoons salt

3 tablespoons tomato paste
dissolved in ½ cup water

3 large fresh green jalapeño
chiles, quartered lengthwise

1½ pounds spinach, with stems
and roots, washed very well

3 ounces capers

1 Preserved Lemon (at right),
quartered

Makes 4 servings

In this Tunisian dish called *tajin marqa mua'lla*, beef is braised with tomato sauce and spices, and then at the very end of the cooking, spinach is wilted into the casserole. The heat of the chile-flavored beef acquires an additional level of tangy flavor from the preserved lemons and capers. The Arabic name of the dish indicates that it is a ragout made with young vegetables in an earthenware casserole, but you can use any casserole you might have to prepare it. Serve with steamed couscous or Rice Pilaf (page 129).

1. In a casserole or stockpot, heat the olive oil over medium-high heat, then brown the beef with the beef bone, onion, cayenne pepper, coriander, and salt, stirring frequently, about 5 minutes. Pour the tomato paste dissolved in water over the meat. Add the fresh chiles.

2. Reduce the heat to low and simmer, partially covered and stirring occasionally, until the beef is tender, 1½ to 2 hours. Add water if it is drying out. Remove the beef bone, scoop the marrow out, and add it to the broth. Discard the bone.

3. Add the spinach, capers, and preserved lemon, stir to mix well, and cook until the spinach has wilted, 8 to 10 minutes. Serve immediately.

Preserved Lemon

Makes 2 preserved lemons

This is one of the most refreshing condiments used anywhere. Although it is typically used in Tunisian cooking, I find myself relying on preserved lemons when I make other kinds of foods and want a particular zestiness. It's easy to prepare, easy to store, and easy to use.

2 thin-skinned Meyer lemons, washed well, dried,
and cut into 8 wedges

⅓ cup salt

½ cup fresh lemon juice

Extra-virgin olive oil, as needed

In a small bowl, toss the lemon wedges with the salt. Place the lemons in a ½-pint jar with a glass or plastic lid, as metal will corrode. Cover the lemons with the lemon juice and screw on the lid. Leave the jar at room temperature for 7 days, shaking it occasionally. After 1 week, pour in olive oil to cover. Store in the refrigerator for up to 6 months.

Beef in Coconut and Chile Curry

4 shallots, coarsely chopped

3 large garlic cloves, chopped

One 1-inch cube fresh ginger, peeled and chopped

3 fresh red finger-type chiles or 4 fresh red jalapeño chiles

2 cups coconut cream (see page 21)

½ lemongrass stalk, tough outer portion removed, white tender part only, finely chopped

One 1-inch cube fresh galangal, peeled and chopped, or one ½-inch cube fresh ginger, peeled and chopped, or ½ teaspoon ground galangal or ¼ teaspoon ground ginger

3 curry leaves (see page 123)

2 teaspoons cayenne pepper or ground red chile

1½ teaspoons salt

1 teaspoon ground coriander

½ teaspoon ground turmeric

1½ pounds beef chuck, cut into 1 x 2-inch strips

1½ tablespoons tamarind paste dissolved in 3 tablespoons hot water

1 teaspoon palm sugar or brown sugar

Makes 4 servings

Rendang daging is an example of a style of cooking in Indonesia called *nasi Padang*, "Padang food." It originates from the western Sumatra province and is named after the capital, Padang. The region is inhabited by the Minangkabau, a Muslim people who are known for raising water buffalo. (For authenticity, you would make this with water buffalo meat.) Even by Indonesian standards, Padang food is quite spicy. *Rendang* is also a popular dish in Malaysia, where it is made for special occasions such as Malaysian New Year or, among Muslims, the Id al-Fitr feast celebrating the breaking of the Ramadan fast. This is an easy dish to make since everything goes into a pot and you cook it with a minimum of fuss. Serve with white rice, one or two vegetables, such as Spicy Cabbage in Coconut Milk (page 123), a variety of sambals (opposite), and prawn crackers, which are sold in many different Asian markets and some supermarkets.

1. Put the shallots, garlic, 1-inch cube ginger, fresh chiles, and ½ cup of the coconut cream into a blender and puree until smooth.

2. Pour the mixture from the blender into a wok or stockpot. Pour the remaining 1½ cups coconut cream into the blender, swish it around, and then pour it into the wok. Add the lemongrass, galangal, curry leaves, cayenne pepper, salt, coriander, and turmeric to the wok. Mix well and add the beef. Bring to a boil over high heat, then reduce the heat to medium and add the tamarind water and cook 1 minute. Reduce the heat to low and simmer, uncovered, stirring occasionally, until the sauce is a thick gravy and almost sticking to the bottom, 3 to 3½ hours. Once the oil of the coconut starts to separate from the gravy, add the sugar, stir, and cook 5 minutes. Serve immediately.

Sambal Ulek

Makes ¼ cup

This is the simplest of the sambals used for Malaysian foods. You can make it by pounding it in a mortar or by putting it in a small food processor. The mortar will work best. As it is a very strongly flavored condiment, use only about ½ to 1 teaspoon per person in a prepared dish. One does not eat this on its own.

Place the chiles, shrimp paste, and salt in a mortar and pound until mushy. Add the tamarind juice and continue pounding until blended. Alternatively, grind in a mini food processor. Store in the refrigerator for several weeks.

12 dried chiles de árbol, stems removed, soaked in water for 30 minutes, drained, and chopped

½ teaspoon shrimp paste

½ teaspoon salt

1 tablespoon tamarind juice or brown sugar

Crying Tiger

Makes 4 servings

Su-Mei Yu, author of *Cracking the Coconut: Classic Thai Home Cooking* (William Morrow, 2000), tells us that this dish of grilled beef with chile dipping sauce called *seua rong hai* is a true Bangkok creation because of its intense flavors. The literal translation is "as the tiger weeps," and it has been suggested that the name comes from how the beef fat "weeps" into the red-hot coals of the grill. But I believe that the reference is probably related to the heat of the chiles, which will indeed make you sweat and tear. It is called "Crying Tiger" because the chiles should be hot enough to make one howl like a tiger, but balanced with a blend of sweet-salty flavors to lessen the fire. The dipping sauce is a kind of *nam prik* (page 22), of which there are many varieties. This dish is nice accompanied by steamed jasmine rice.

1. In a large bowl, combine the soy sauce, 2 tablespoons of the fish sauce, and the sugar. Stir until the sugar dissolves. Place the steak in the bowl, turn several times, and marinate for 1 hour at room temperature, turning once.

2. Meanwhile, preheat the oven to 400°F. Cut the garlic heads in half so the inside of the cloves are exposed and drizzle with the vegetable oil, then wrap in aluminum foil and roast until the insides are soft, 30 minutes. Cool, then squeeze the soft garlic mush from the skins into a small bowl and set aside.

3. Prepare a hot charcoal fire or preheat a gas grill on high for 15 minutes.

4. Meanwhile, prepare the dipping sauce. In a small cast-iron skillet, dry-roast the chiles over high heat with the salt, shaking the skillet, until the chiles begin to blacken, 3 to 4 minutes. Remove and cool. Transfer garlic and chiles to a food processor along with the shallot, cilantro, and galangal and puree into a paste. Add the remaining 2 tablespoons fish sauce and the lime juice and continue to puree, scraping down the sides when necessary, about 3 minutes of continuous processing. Transfer to a small bowl for dipping.

5. Place the steak on the grill, 4 to 5 inches directly above a very hot fire, and cook, turning several times, until the center is medium rare, 8 to 10 minutes. If you are using the rib eye, which is marbled with more fat, it will flare up more than the London broil and char the steak a bit, which is preferred for this dish. Remove the steak from the grill and transfer to a carving or serving platter and let it rest 10 minutes. Slice crosswise into thin slices and serve with the dipping sauce.

¼ cup soy sauce

¼ cup Thai fish sauce

1 tablespoon palm sugar or granulated sugar

1 pound beef rib eye or beef round (London broil), in 1 piece

2 heads garlic

2 teaspoons vegetable oil

¼ cup dried bird's eye chiles or dried piquín chiles or crumbled dried chiles de árbol

½ teaspoon salt

1 shallot, chopped

1 tablespoon finely chopped fresh cilantro leaves

One 1-inch cube fresh galangal or ginger, peeled and chopped

3 tablespoons fresh lime juice

Chili con Carne

2 tablespoons bacon drippings or rendered beef kidney suet

3 pounds boneless beef chuck, trimmed of fat, chopped in a food processor by pulsing or chopped into ¼-inch dice, but not ground

4 tablespoons dark chili powder

2 teaspoons granulated garlic

6 dried pasilla chiles or dried ancho chiles

1 dried New Mexico chile (also called Anaheim, long green, or long red chiles)

2 dried guajillo (mirasol) chiles

2 cups cold water

3 cups beef broth (homemade or store-bought)

2 large garlic cloves, crushed

2 tablespoons onion powder

1½ tablespoons garlic powder

1 tablespoon gently crushed cumin seeds or ground cumin

1 tablespoon hot paprika

2 teaspoons cayenne pepper

2 teaspoons freshly ground white pepper

1 teaspoon ground red chile

1 tablespoon dried oregano

1 teaspoon salt

2 cups lager beer (such as Corona)

(continued)

Makes 6 servings

This chili con carne recipe was first published in my book *Real Stew* (The Harvard Common Press, 2002). It's just great, so I'm not going to tweak it at all. Let me reprise here what I said there: Chili con carne is not a Mexican dish. It is a classic, defining dish of Texas cooking. A true Texas "bowl of red" contains neither beans nor tomatoes, the purists say. Another element of a true chili is that it is made with finely diced beef chuck, not ground beef. In Texas one drinks beer with chili con carne. All the chiles mentioned here, by the way, are easily found in Texas and west to California, but perhaps less so in the rest of the country. Serve this chili with cornbread, flour tortillas, or corn tortillas . . . and beer.

1. In a large casserole or Dutch oven, heat the bacon fat over medium-high heat, then brown the meat with 2 tablespoons of the chili powder and the granulated garlic, in batches if necessary, about 5 minutes. Turn the heat off and return all the cooked beef to the casserole if you cooked in batches.

2. Place the pasilla, New Mexico, and guajillo chiles in a small saucepan with the water. Bring to a gentle boil over medium-high heat, reduce the heat to low, and simmer until soft, 20 minutes, covered. Drain the chiles, reserving the cooking water. Place the chiles in a food processor with 2 to 4 tablespoons of the reserved cooking water and puree until a smooth paste forms and there is no evidence of any pieces of pepper skin. Mix the chile puree into the beef, add 2 cups of the beef broth, and bring to a boil over high heat. Reduce the heat to low, cover, and gently simmer for 30 minutes.

3. Stir the crushed garlic, onion powder, garlic powder, cumin, paprika, cayenne pepper, white pepper, ground red chile, oregano, salt, and the remaining 2 tablespoons dark chili powder, beer, and the remaining 1 cup beef broth into the casserole. Bring to a boil over high heat, then reduce the heat to low and add the serrano chiles, vinegar, chocolate, brown sugar, and Tabasco. Cover and simmer 45 minutes.

4. In a small bowl, stir a ladleful of broth with the masa harina until there are no lumps and then pour into the casserole. Cook uncovered on the lowest possible heat, using a heat diffuser if necessary and stirring occasionally so that the mixture doesn't stick, until the meat is very tender and the gravy is thick, 1½ to 2 hours. If the chili con carne is too thick, thin it with small amounts of boiling water. Serve immediately, or refrigerate it overnight and serve it the next day after a minute of microwaving.

4 fresh green serrano chiles, seeded and chopped

2 tablespoons red wine vinegar

2 tablespoons shaved bitter chocolate or unsweetened cocoa powder

1 tablespoon brown sugar

½ teaspoon Tabasco sauce

¼ cup masa harina (Mexican corn flour)

Lamb in Spicy Cardamom
and Rose Water–Flavored Yogurt Sauce

2 pounds boneless lamb shoulder or lamb top round, excess fat removed, cut into 1-inch cubes

Salt to taste

2 cups Stabilized Yogurt (opposite)

2 teaspoons freshly and finely ground white pepper

¼ cup raw, unsalted cashews or whole blanched almonds

1 ounce fresh coconut flesh (from ½ small coconut) or 1 cup dried unsweetened shredded coconut

3 tablespoons vegetable oil

2 tablespoons julienned fresh ginger

1½ cups water

¾ teaspoon freshly and finely ground white cardamom seeds

¼ cup heavy cream

Juice from 1 lemon

4 fresh green finger-type chiles or 5 fresh green jalapeño chiles, seeded and chopped

2 teaspoons rose water

Makes 4 to 6 servings

This rich dish, called *safed maas*, from Rajasthan belies the stark and arid landscape of this mostly desert state in northwest India. This dish is not only hot from chiles but also fragrant from coconut, ginger, rose water, and cardamom. It should be served with rice and Mustard Greens and Chiles (page 171). Both the white pepper and cardamom should ideally be freshly ground, and the coconut should ideally be fresh.

1. Put the lamb and water to cover in a large saucepan, add salt to taste, and bring to a boil. Boil the lamb for 5 minutes. Drain and rinse the lamb.

2. As the lamb cooks, in a small bowl, whisk the yogurt until smooth, then add the white pepper and mix again. Place the cashews and coconut in a food processor and blend until a paste forms.

3. In a large skillet, heat the vegetable oil over medium-high heat, then add the lamb, yogurt mixture, ginger, salt to taste, and the 1½ cups water. Cover, reduce the heat to low, and simmer, stirring occasionally, until the lamb is tender, 2½ to 3 hours.

4. Add the cashew-coconut mixture to the lamb and stir for 2 minutes. Sprinkle in the cardamom and stir. Add the cream, lemon juice, chiles, and rose water and stir. Cover the pan and cook over low heat until the sauce is thick and syrupy, about 15 minutes. Serve immediately.

Stabilized Yogurt

Makes 1 quart

Stabilized yogurt is yogurt that is cooked for several minutes. Sometimes this is necessary before using cow's milk yogurt in cooking, because otherwise it will separate if heated beyond a certain point.

In a saucepan, beat the yogurt with a fork until smooth, then beat in the egg white, cornstarch, and salt. Put the saucepan over high heat and start stirring in one direction with a wooden spoon. As soon as it starts to bubble, after about 6 minutes, reduce the heat to medium and boil gently until it is thick, about 5 minutes. Set aside until needed. Stabilized yogurt will keep in the refrigerator for up to 3 weeks.

1 quart whole plain yogurt

1 large egg white, beaten

1 tablespoon cornstarch

1 teaspoon salt

Lamb and Pumpkin Curry

🌶 🌶 🌶 🌶

1 pound boneless leg of lamb, cut into 1-inch cubes

2 tablespoons curry powder

Salt to taste

1 teaspoon ground allspice

1 teaspoon freshly ground black pepper

1 teaspoon ground coriander

2 tablespoons vegetable oil

1 medium-size onion, chopped

3 large garlic cloves, finely chopped

2 pounds tomatoes, cut in half, seeds squeezed out, and grated against the largest holes of a grater

1 tablespoon tomato paste

6 ounces diced pumpkin or other winter squash flesh

1 fresh Scotch bonnet chile or fresh habanero chile, finely chopped

½ cup beef broth (homemade or store-bought)

2 sprigs fresh thyme

2 tablespoons finely chopped fresh cilantro leaves (optional)

Makes 4 servings

Curry came to Jamaica with East Indian workers who immigrated there in the late nineteenth century, after the abolition of slavery. They worked on the plantations, and their curries from India were transformed into super-hot dishes such as this Jamaican lamb stew. You will want to eat it with something very bland, such as plantains or white rice.

1. In a large bowl, toss the lamb with the curry powder, salt, allspice, black pepper, and ground coriander and leave in the refrigerator, covered with plastic wrap, for 2 hours.

2. In a large stockpot or casserole, heat the vegetable oil over medium-high heat, then brown the lamb, turning and tossing it, about 6 minutes. Add the onion, garlic, tomatoes, and tomato paste and cook, stirring, for 5 minutes. Add the pumpkin, chile, beef broth, thyme, and cilantro, if using. Stir well, reduce the heat to low, cover, and simmer, using a heat diffuser if necessary, until the lamb is tender and the pumpkin is very soft, 2½ to 3 hours. Serve immediately.

Lamb Keema

2 pounds ground lamb

5 fresh green finger-type chiles
or 6 fresh green jalapeño chiles,
seeded and finely chopped

4 large garlic cloves, pounded in
a mortar with 1 teaspoon salt
until mushy

4 teaspoons very finely chopped
ginger

1 large egg

2 tablespoons fresh breadcrumbs

1 tablespoon white wine vinegar

2 teaspoons ground cumin

1 teaspoon ground red chile or
cayenne pepper

¼ cup vegetable oil

1 small lemon, thinly sliced, for
garnish

3 tablespoons chopped fresh
cilantro leaves, for garnish

Makes 4 servings

A lamb keema is a ground lamb dish. This dish is from Lucknow in the state of Uttar Pradesh, which is famous for its Muslim-influenced keemas, koftas (meatballs), and kebabs. I've adapted this recipe from one by Sanjay Kumar and Nivedita Srivastava. Serve with Rice Pilaf (page 129) or naan.

1. In a large bowl, mix the ground lamb, chiles, garlic and salt, ginger, egg, breadcrumbs, vinegar, cumin, and ground red chile. Let rest for 30 minutes in the refrigerator.

2. In a large skillet, heat the vegetable oil over high heat, then add the ground meat and cook for 1 minute, stirring. Reduce the heat to low, cover, and cook, stirring occasionally, until browned and tender, about 1 hour. Remove from the heat, arrange on a serving platter, and garnish with the lemon and cilantro. Serve immediately.

Chapter 3

PIQUANT
Pork

Pork Vindaloo

2 pounds boneless pork loin, fat removed and cut into 1-inch cubes

Salt to taste

20 dried chiles de árbol, broken in half and seeded

10 black peppercorns

8 whole cloves

1 cinnamon stick

1 teaspoon cumin seeds

1 teaspoon coriander seeds

½ teaspoon black mustard seeds

1 teaspoon ground turmeric

One 1-inch cube fresh ginger, peeled

6 large garlic cloves

1 teaspoon sugar

½ cup apple cider vinegar

2 tablespoons vegetable oil

2 medium-size onions, finely chopped

2 large tomatoes, peeled, seeded, and chopped

6 fresh green finger-style chiles or 8 fresh green jalapeño chiles or 12 fresh green serrano chiles, sliced

¾ cup coconut milk (see box on page 21)

Makes 6 servings

This famous dish from Goa in western India takes its name from the Portuguese, who held Goa as a colony for about 450 years, until 1961. The word *vindaloo* derives from the Portuguese words *vinho* for wine and *alhos* for garlic. Goa's Hindu community tends to make vindaloo with seafood, while pork is popular with Goa's Christian community. The Christian community uses vinegar in its cooking while the Hindus use tamarind. Some Goan cooks use *feni*, a distilled drink made from coconut sap, in the vinegar sauce. In Goa and all of India, the dried red chiles used are called Kashmiri chiles, because that is where most of them come from, but chiles de árbol are a good substitute. Serve with Rice Pilaf (page 129).

1. Sprinkle the pork with salt and set aside in a large bowl. Place the dried chiles, peppercorns, cloves, cinnamon stick, cumin seeds, coriander seeds, mustard seeds, and turmeric in a spice mill and grind to a powder. Transfer the spice mix to a blender with the ginger, garlic, sugar, and vinegar and blend. Pour the mixture over the pork, toss, cover, and marinate in the refrigerator for 4 to 6 hours.

2. In a wok or large skillet, heat the vegetable oil over medium heat, then cook the pork with its marinade for 5 minutes. Add the onions, tomatoes, fresh chiles, and coconut milk. Cover, reduce the heat to low, and cook, stirring occasionally, until the meat is tender, 30 to 35 minutes. If the sauce is liquidy, remove the meat with a skimmer and set it aside while you reduce the sauce over high heat until thickened, 10 to 15 minutes. Return the meat to the sauce and cook until heated through, about 3 minutes. Serve immediately.

Chile Verde

Makes 4 to 6 servings

Chile verde could be considered the state dish of New Mexico. New Mexico cooking is distinct from Tex-Mex and from Cal-Mex, and it is redolent with the smells and tastes of the Southwest, especially that combination of pork, New Mexico chiles, and chipotle chiles. This recipe comes from my friend Chris Hardy, whose grandmother is a native of New Mexico. I first published this recipe in my book *Real Stew* (The Harvard Common Press, 2002), and am only fine tuning it here. Serve the stew with little side dishes of chopped onion, chopped cilantro, sour cream or Mexican crema, *panela* and cotija cheese (see www.caciquefoods.com), or queso fresco, ricotta salata, or mild domestic feta cheese to crumble over the top. For accompaniment, white rice, refried black beans cooked with epazote (see box on page 17), corn tortillas, and good Mexican beer are all traditional. If you'd like it hotter, add a little of the sauce from a can of chipotle chiles in adobo.

1. Preheat the oven to 450°F. Place the fresh chiles on a baking sheet and roast until the skin blisters and turns black, 25 to 30 minutes, watching them carefully. Remove and place in a paper bag to steam for 10 minutes. Remove and, when the chiles are cool enough to handle, peel, stem, seed, and cut into strips. Alternatively, roast the chiles directly over a cooktop burner.

2. In a large casserole or Dutch oven, heat 2 tablespoons of the olive oil over medium heat, then cook the onion and garlic, stirring, until translucent, about 8 minutes. Remove and set aside. Add 1 tablespoon olive oil to the casserole and let it heat up. Dredge the pork in the masa harina. Tap off any excess, then brown the pork on all sides over medium heat, cooking in two batches if necessary so the pieces of meat don't touch each other, about 12 minutes for each batch, turning with tongs. Use the remaining 1 tablespoon olive oil for the second batch. Set the meat aside.

3. Deglaze the bottom of the casserole by pouring in about a quarter of the beer, scraping up the bits on the bottom with a wooden spoon. Once all the crust is picked up, add the remaining beer. Return the onion and garlic and pork to the casserole. Add the cumin and cook on medium-low heat for 10 minutes. Add the roasted chile strips, chipotle chiles in adobo, bay leaf, oregano, and the salt and black pepper. Bring to a boil over high heat, reduce the heat to low, cover, and cook, stirring occasionally, until the pork is very tender, about 45 minutes. Add the cilantro and cook for another 10 minutes, then turn the heat off and let it sit for 5 minutes before serving.

10 fresh New Mexico chiles

4 tablespoons extra-virgin olive oil

1 large onion, coarsely chopped

4 large garlic cloves, passed through a garlic press or mashed in a mortar

2 pounds boneless pork shoulder or butt, as much fat removed as possible, cut into 1-inch cubes

Masa harina (corn flour), for dredging

1½ cups lager beer

1 teaspoon ground cumin

3 tablespoons chopped chipotle chiles in adobo

1 bay leaf

1 tablespoon dried oregano

2 teaspoons salt

2 teaspoons freshly ground black pepper

½ cup coarsely chopped fresh cilantro leaves

Pork
with Chipotle Chile Cream Sauce

¼ cup finely chopped fresh parsley leaves

¼ cup finely chopped fresh cilantro leaves

2 tablespoons fresh lime juice

1 large garlic clove, finely chopped

Salt and freshly ground black pepper to taste

2¾ pounds boneless pork shoulder, in 1 piece

1 tablespoon lard or vegetable oil (if needed)

3 canned chipotle chiles in adobo

1 cup crème fraîche or sour cream

¼ cup shredded Monterey Jack cheese or Mexican queso asadero

¼ cup shredded white cheddar cheese or Mexican queso blanco

Makes 4 servings

The mixture of a rich, mild cream with blazing-hot smoked jalapeño chiles, which are what chipotle chiles are, is so appealing in taste because, I believe, they balance each other so well. This recipe, called *carne de puerco con chipotle*, is adapted from the *Larousse Mexican Cookbook* (Larousse, 1984) by Sue Style. Serve this with white rice and cooked spinach.

1. In a small bowl, mix the parsley, cilantro, lime juice, garlic, and salt and black pepper. Rub the mixture all over the pork and place in a small or medium pot that will fit the pork relatively snugly. Let marinate for 6 hours in the refrigerator.

2. Pour in enough water to cover the pork by an inch, bring to a boil over high heat, and cook at a boil, uncovered, until the liquid has evaporated and the meat is starting to fry in its own fat, about 1 hour. Cover with water again, bring to a boil again, and continue boiling until the water has evaporated and the pork is tender, about another hour. Add the lard only if there isn't enough fat to fry the pork. Once all the liquid has evaporated, let the pork brown all over in the fat at the bottom of the casserole, about 4 minutes. Remove the meat to a cutting board or platter and let it rest for 10 minutes. Slice the pork off the bone; discard any gristle, excessive fat, and skin; and slice the meat into ½-inch slices.

3. Meanwhile, preheat the oven to 350°F. In a food processor or blender, blend the chipotle chiles, crème fraîche, and salt to taste together until smooth. Arrange the pork slices in a baking dish and spread the sauce over it. Sprinkle on both cheeses and bake until the cheese is bubbling and melted, about 30 minutes. Serve immediately.

Pork Adobo

1¼ pounds boneless pork shoulder, cut into ½-inch cubes

½ teaspoon ground annatto (achiote) seeds

3 large garlic cloves, finely chopped

1 teaspoon freshly ground black pepper, or more to your taste

½ teaspoon ground cumin

½ cup white vinegar

1 medium-size onion, halved and cut into ¼-inch slices

¼ cup Aji Panca en Pasta (opposite)

2 tablespoons safflower oil

2 teaspoons salt

Makes 4 servings

This marinated Peruvian dish is called *adobo de cerdo* and is made with *ají panca en pasta*, a paste made from a Peruvian chile whose pungency is considered mild, or so a Peruvian tells me. One man's mild is another man's fire. This chile will not be found in your supermarkets, so you will need to order it online or substitute the combination I suggest below. Serve this with white rice and boiled sweet potatoes, cassava, or white potatoes.

1. Place the pork in a large bowl with the annatto, half of the garlic, the black pepper, and cumin. Toss well, then add the vinegar, onion, and aji panca en pasta. Toss and stir again to combine all the ingredients. Cover and marinate in the refrigerator for 24 hours.

2. In a large skillet, heat the oil over medium-high heat, then cook the remaining garlic for a few seconds, until sizzling. Add the pork and its marinade, including the onion. Stir, add the salt and more black pepper if desired, and stir again. Cover, reduce the heat to low, and cook, stirring occasionally, until the pork is tender, about 2 hours. Add small amounts of water if necessary to keep the meat from drying out. Serve immediately.

Ají Panca en Pasta

Makes about 1¼ cups

Ají panca is the name of a particular Peruvian chile that is considered to be of mild pungency; nevertheless, by any measure, it is still a hot chile. It grows up to 5 inches long and when it is ripe it is nearly deep red to purple in color, and at that time it is picked and sun-dried. This chile paste is a kind of South American Harissa and is used as a condiment in a variety of Peruvian dishes. It is made by soaking the dried chiles in water and then blending them into a paste. Some Peruvian cooks also boil the dried chiles. As this South American chile is available only on the Internet at this time, I make some suggestions for substitutes.

In a bowl, soak the dried chiles in warm water to cover until very soft, 3 to 5 hours. Remove and place in a food processor with the fresh chiles, cumin, salt, and oil. Puree until smooth, about 2 minutes. Transfer to a jar or container and refrigerate until needed, up to 1 month.

10 dried ají panca chiles or a combination of 3 dried pasilla chiles, 3 dried guajillo chiles, and 8 dried chiles de árbol

2 fresh ají panca chiles or fresh red jalapeño chiles, stems removed

½ teaspoon ground cumin

½ teaspoon salt

1 tablespoon safflower oil

Carnitas

Makes 8 servings

This absolutely delicious crisp-on-the-outside, succulent-on-the-inside pork dish is traditionally made from pork butt or the thick, meaty cut called pork country ribs. The final result is meat that is orange-tinged from chipotle chiles in adobo, soft and succulent from hours of stewing in a flavorful broth, and crispy on the outside after roasting in a hot oven. Carnitas can be eaten as is or—and this is preferable—wrapped in tortillas with guacamole, black beans, and/or white rice. This is a meal that you are very likely to find at roadside stands throughout Mexico.

1. Place the pork in a large stockpot or Dutch oven. Add the onion, chipotle, adobo sauce, bay leaves, cumin, coriander, oregano, salt, and 2 quarts chicken broth. If the pork is not covered with liquid, add more chicken broth. Cover the pot and bring to a boil over high heat. Reduce the heat to low, uncover, and simmer until the meat pulls apart easily with a fork, about 3 hours. Remove the pork from the broth with a slotted spoon and place on a platter. Allow to cool, then cut into 1-inch cubes.

2. Preheat the oven to 450°F. Place the lard in a baking dish and melt in the oven. Toss the pork in the lard, then roast in the oven, uncovered, until lightly browned and sizzling, about 30 minutes. Remove and serve.

One 7-pound pork butt, cut into 10 large chunks

1 very large onion, quartered

5 canned chipotle chiles in adobo, chopped, plus 3 tablespoons adobo sauce from the can

2 bay leaves

1 tablespoon ground cumin

1 tablespoon ground coriander

1 tablespoon dried oregano

1 tablespoon salt

2 to 3 quarts chicken broth (homemade or store-bought), or more as needed

2 tablespoons lard or vegetable oil

Jerk Pork

For the Jerk Marinade

2 tablespoons ground allspice

2 tablespoons dried thyme

2 tablespoons salt

1 tablespoon cayenne pepper

1 tablespoon freshly ground black pepper

1 tablespoon dried sage

1 tablespoon sugar

1½ teaspoons ground nutmeg

1½ teaspoons ground cinnamon

6 large garlic cloves

One 1-inch cube fresh ginger, peeled

½ bunch fresh cilantro, leaves only

¾ cup fresh lime juice

½ cup fresh orange juice

¼ cup soy sauce

¼ cup peanut oil

2 cups chopped scallions

8 fresh Scotch bonnet chiles or fresh habanero chiles, stemmed and finely chopped

3 pounds boneless pork loin or 4 pounds boneless pork shoulder, cut into 1-pound chunks and scored in a diamond pattern 1½ inches apart

Oil, for the grill

Makes 6 to 8 servings

Jerk is a Jamaican technique for slow- and well-cooked spiced meat that results in a smoky, pungent, succulent preparation. This recipe is the real thing—if you love flavorful hot food this is the recipe you must make. The beginning point of a jerk is a complex marinade that always includes the native spice known as allspice (called pimento in Jamaica). Jerk marinade also includes a good amount of Scotch bonnet chile and some combination of thyme, scallions, ginger, garlic, and nutmeg as well as other ingredients such as sage, cinnamon, nutmeg, cloves, orange juice, lime juice, soy sauce, and coriander. In Jamaica, the meat is cooked with the highly aromatic wood and leaves of the pimento (allspice) tree. You can also use another aromatic wood to cook the meat, such as apple, hickory, birch, pecan, or oak, but not mesquite.

Jerk pork can be made with pork loin or tenderloin or with shoulder. I prefer shoulder because it is fattier and juicier, and loin can, if you are not careful, overcook easily. Depending on which cut you choose, the cooking will be different. If you use pork loin the meat will look white when it is done, and if you use shoulder the meat will be reddish, almost like beef. The trickiest part of the cooking is grilling at a low enough temperature—about 225°F—for 2½ to 3 hours and up to 5 hours, until the internal temperature of the pork is about 135°F for loin and up to 160°F for shoulder. Realistically, you should assume your grill will be too hot and that you should check the pork for doneness in about 2 hours. An accurate meat thermometer is very useful here; if the meat is cooking too quickly, set it as far away from the fire as possible and remove the cover. Serve with a simple coleslaw.

1. Place the jerk marinade ingredients in a blender and run until smooth. Place the pork pieces in a large ceramic or glass dish and pour the marinade over the pork, coating well. Cover with plastic wrap and marinate in the refrigerator for 1½ days. Alternatively, place the meat and its marinade in two zip-top plastic bags to marinate.

2. Prepare a small, hot charcoal fire, or preheat only one set of burners on a gas grill on low for 15 minutes. Push the coals to one side of the grill, preferably the side with a latched opening so you can add coals occasionally if necessary, and let the fire die down a bit. Remove the pork from the marinade and reserve the marinade. Place the pork on the side away from the fire, directly on oiled grilling grates or in an aluminum roasting pan, and grill slowly, turning and basting with the remaining marinade every 20 minutes, until blackened on the outside and cooked through, with an internal temperature of 135° to 140°F for the pork loin and 155° to 160°F for the pork shoulder, 2½ to 5 hours. Remove the pork from the grill, let sit 5 minutes, then cut into thin slices and serve.

Bhutan Pork
with Bean Threads and Chile

2 ounces bean threads or
  cellophane noodles

½ cup (1 stick) unsalted butter

1 medium-size onion, chopped

1 medium-size tomato, peeled
  and chopped

1½ pounds boneless pork
  shoulder, cut into 1-inch cubes

½ cup water

3 fresh green finger-type chiles
  or 4 fresh green jalapeño
  chiles, seeded and julienned

1½ teaspoons salt, or more to your
  taste

Freshly ground black pepper to
  taste

Makes 6 servings

Bhutan is a small, primarily Buddhist, Himalayan country between India
and China. The country is under the protectorship of India, and it is
from India that the first chiles arrived in Bhutan. They are a favorite
ingredient in Bhutanese cuisine. Here they add zest to a mellow pork
and noodle combination called *fing*. This recipe is adapted from Susanne
Waugh, a traveler to Bhutan in the early 1980s who collected recipes. I
make this with some frequency because it is rich in chile flavor and also
quite easy.

1. Bring a small saucepan filled with water to a boil and cook the bean
threads for 2 minutes. Drain and snip into 6-inch lengths with kitchen
scissors.

2. In a large saucepan or casserole, melt the butter over medium-high heat,
then add the onion, tomato, pork, and water. Bring to just below a boil, then
reduce the heat to low and cook, partially covered, until just tender, about 1½
hours. Add the bean threads, chiles, and salt and black pepper to taste and
simmer until heated through, about 10 minutes.

Variation Add 1 pound bok choy, split lengthwise into quarters or sixths, at
the same time you add the pork.

Jamaican Roast Pork

3 pounds boneless pork shoulder, in 1 piece

5 large garlic cloves, 3 slivered and 2 finely chopped

3 tablespoons vegetable oil

4 fresh Scotch bonnet chiles or fresh habanero chiles, seeded and chopped

1 green bell pepper, coarsely chopped

1 medium-size onion, coarsely chopped

1 teaspoon ground cumin

1 teaspoon dried oregano

1 teaspoon freshly ground black pepper

½ teaspoon ground cinnamon

1 bay leaf

½ cup fresh lime juice

2 cups canned or fresh tomato puree

Makes 6 servings

After you taste this you will see why pork is a popular meat in Jamaica. Yes, this is blazingly hot, but the pork is so tender after all the roasting that it just melts in your mouth. This dish is thought to have been influenced by the Spanish, who probably added the tomatoes to the recipe. Although you don't have to, pushing the sauce through a food mill until it is smooth is a nice finishing touch. Serve with Fried Plantains (page 69) and plain rice.

1. Make slits all over the pork with the tip of a paring knife and stuff them with the slivered garlic. Roll up the pork and tie with kitchen twine.

2. To make the marinade, in a large skillet, heat the vegetable oil over medium-high heat. Cook the chiles, bell pepper, onion, chopped garlic, cumin, oregano, black pepper, cinnamon, and bay leaf, stirring frequently, until the vegetables are soft, about 8 minutes. Remove the skillet from the heat and stir in the lime juice.

3. Place the pork in a large bowl and pour the marinade over it, turning the meat several times to coat it evenly. Cover with plastic wrap and refrigerate, turning occasionally, for 2 to 8 hours.

4. Preheat the oven to 350°F. Scrape the marinade off the pork and reserve in a saucepan. Place the pork in a roasting pan and roast until a meat thermometer registers 165°F, about 1¾ hours. Meanwhile, add the tomato puree to the marinade and bring it, stirring, almost to a boil. Before it begins to sputter too much, reduce the heat to low and simmer for 5 minutes. Remove the bay leaf and pass the sauce through a food mill if desired. Transfer the pork to a serving platter and let stand 10 minutes. Slice the pork, spoon the sauce over, and serve immediately.

Fried Plantains

Makes 4 to 6 servings

You will want to make this recipe as an accompaniment to any hot dishes from the Caribbean or Africa. This method of cooking the plantains is really the one that works the best. "Green" means the plantain is not ripe.

1. In a small skillet, heat the vegetable oil over medium heat, then cook the plantain pieces, four at a time, turning with tongs, until golden on all sides, 5 to 6 minutes. Reduce the heat if they are cooking more quickly. Remove the plantains from the oil and carefully and gently pound them with a rolling pin or the side of a cleaver until flattened to ⅜ inch thick. Set aside and continue cooking and pounding the remaining pieces, adding more oil to the skillet if necessary.

2. Remove to a paper towel–lined baking dish and season with salt. You can serve them immediately, keep them warm in an oven, or serve them at room temperature.

½ cup vegetable oil, plus more as needed

3 large green plantains, peeled and cut into 2-inch lengths

Salt to taste

Chile Oil ✈ ✈ ✈ ✈ ✈

Makes 1 quart l

The best way to make this chile oil is with a large bag of bright red dried chiles de árbol. There's one thing you need to be very careful about when doing this—and I learned the hard way through carelessness. When the chiles hit the oil at such a high temperature, they will release their pungent, irritating fumes, and if you are facing the oil it will hit you smack in the eyes and nose. This is not fun, so turn the exhaust fan to high and look and lean away from the oil as you do it. This oil is used in Sichuan and Thai cooking, but it's great for anything.

In a wok, heat the peanut oil over high heat. Once it starts to smoke, add the red pepper flakes and turn the heat off. Turn your head away, and do not lean over the wok or try to smell anything at this point. Let cool completely in the wok, and then cover and leave standing for 2 days. Strain the oil through a cheesecloth-lined sieve into a clean, dry storage bottle and discard the flakes. Store in a dark, cool place as you would other oils.

4 cups peanut oil

1½ cups red pepper flakes (chiles de árbol)

Pork and Peanuts

in Hot and Spicy Sauce

Makes 4 servings

This pork dish from Sichuan is moist and golden, punctuated by nearly blackened dry red chiles. It's a delicious and very hot preparation that should be savored slowly with some steamed rice on the side.

1. In a small skillet, heat the peanut oil over high heat, then fry the peanuts until golden brown, about 30 seconds or less, stirring. Remove and cool the peanuts.

2. In a medium bowl, toss the pork cubes with 1 teaspoon salt. In a large bowl, beat the egg whites until they form peaks, then mix with 2 tablespoons of the cornstarch. Add the pork cubes, mix well, and set aside.

3. To make the sauce, in a small bowl, mix the beef broth with the remaining ½ tablespoon (1½ teaspoons) cornstarch, remaining ½ teaspoon salt, the scallions, garlic, rice wine, soy sauce, ginger, and sugar and set aside.

4. In a wok, heat 5 tablespoons of the vegetable oil over medium-high heat, then cook the pork and egg white mixture until the pork turns color and the egg whites solidify into smaller light golden pieces, 1 to 2 minutes. Remove with a skimmer and set aside. Add the chiles to the wok and cook until they begin to darken, about 30 seconds. Remove and set the chiles aside with the pork. Add the remaining 1 tablespoon vegetable oil to the wok and heat over high heat. Add the green pepper and stir-fry for 30 seconds. Return the pork cubes and chiles to the wok and stir-fry for 1 minute. Stir the reserved sauce to blend it, then add to the wok and cook for 1 minute. Add the peanuts and chile oil and cook, stirring and tossing, until thickened. Serve immediately.

¼ cup peanut oil

¼ cup roasted unsalted peanuts

¾ pound boneless pork shoulder, cut into ½-inch cubes

1½ teaspoons salt, or more to your taste

4 large egg whites

2½ tablespoons cornstarch

¼ cup beef broth (homemade or store-bought)

1 tablespoon very finely chopped scallions

2 large garlic cloves, thinly sliced

2 teaspoons rice wine (mirin) or vermouth

2 teaspoons soy sauce

1 teaspoon ground ginger

1 teaspoon sugar

6 tablespoons vegetable oil

¼ cup dried chiles de árbol, cut in half and seeded

1 small green bell pepper, cut into ½-inch squares

2 teaspoons Chile Oil (page 69)

Little Roast Pig

One 5-pound bone-in pork butt or shoulder with its fat

2 teaspoons salt

For the Marinade
3 fresh habanero chiles, finely chopped

8 large garlic cloves, chopped

¼ cup freshly ground black pepper

1 tablespoon ground annatto (achiote) seeds

2 teaspoons dried oregano

1 teaspoon ground cinnamon

1 teaspoon ground cumin

¼ teaspoon hot paprika

3 allspice berries

⅔ cup fresh orange juice, orange rinds reserved

¼ cup red wine vinegar

For the Wrapping
1 large onion, sliced, or reserved orange rind halves

Banana leaves, plantain leaves, or cornhusks

For the Sauce
½ cup very finely chopped onions

3 fresh habanero chiles, very finely chopped

½ teaspoon salt

⅔ cup fresh bitter orange juice or ⅓ cup navel orange juice and ⅓ cup lime juice

Tortillas, for serving

Makes 6 servings

The Mexican name of this famous dish from the Yucatán, *cochinita pibil*, almost literally means "little roast pig." *Pibil* is a Mayan word that refers to the traditional oven of the Yucatán, which was a pit lined with stones where a roaring fire was made and a marinated piglet was wrapped in banana or plantain leaves and cooked in a manner similar to a New England clam bake. In this adaptation, I've used a pork butt and roasted it in the oven. Should you want to give pit-barbecuing a try (without actually digging a pit), build a charcoal fire on one side of your grill, place the wrapped pork on the other side, and grill for many hours, replenishing the coals when necessary. Should you want to roast the pork while you are away at work, set the oven to 250°F and place the roast in by 7:00 A.M. It will be tender and done by 7:00 P.M. You can also cook this in a slow cooker. Read the instructions to your crock pot for timing.

1. Pierce the pork several times with a skewer and rub the salt all over it. Combine the marinade ingredients in a small bowl, then coat the pork with the marinade. Place the onion over the meat, then wrap it up with banana leaves. Refrigerate overnight.

2. Preheat the oven to 325°F. Transfer the wrapped pork to a roasting pan and place in the oven to roast until very tender and the meat shreds easily with a fork, 6 to 7 hours.

3. Meanwhile, to make the sauce, place the onion, habanero chiles, salt, and bitter orange or orange-lime juice mix in a blender and run briefly until almost smooth. Transfer to a serving bowl.

4. When the pork is done, remove the wrapping from the meat and shred the pork off the bone with two forks. Transfer the meat to a serving platter and spoon the collected juices over it. Serve hot with the sauce and tortillas.

Annatto (Achiote) Seeds

The annatto tree (*Bixa orellana*) is a small tree or tall shrub that is native to tropical America. Its small red seeds, called *achiote*, are a much-used spice for coloring and flavoring food in the Yucatán and southern parts of Mexico as well as parts of the Caribbean. They are often used to color butter, cheese, and ointments yellow. Annatto seeds can be found in Latin American markets or online.

Soft Tacos of Pork
and Chile–Sesame Seed Sauce

2 tablespoons lard

2 pounds boneless pork loin, excess fat removed, cut into ¾-inch cubes

1 fresh pasilla chile, roasted, seeded, and chopped

1 fresh poblano chile or fresh jalapeño chile, roasted, seeded, and chopped

1 dried ancho (mulato) chile, soaked in tepid water for 30 minutes, drained, seeded, and chopped

1 canned chipotle chile in adobo, chopped

1 ounce (about 3 tablespoons) sesame seeds, toasted in a toaster oven until light brown

3 ounces (about 1 cup) dried shrimp, soaked in water for 10 minutes and drained

¾ cup water, plus more to thin sauce if needed

½ teaspoon dried oregano

Salt to taste

½ cup sour cream

16 corn tortillas, warmed

Makes 8 servings

In the Mexican states of Oaxaca and Guerrero, this appetizer is known by its Nahuatl name, *pizatl en chitextli*. In Mexican culinary vernacular, an ancho chile is the name of the fresh variety; once dried it's called a *mulato*. But these chile names can become quite confused: for instance, some packagers in southern California sell pasilla/ancho chiles as if they were the same thing, though they're not. In any case, this is a delicious and not-too-hot preparation that should be served as soon as it is cooked. Dried shrimp can be found in some supermarkets in the southwestern United States as well as in Latin and Asian markets throughout the country and on the Internet. Serve with warm corn tortillas on the side for diners to make their own soft tacos.

1. In a large skillet, melt 1 tablespoon lard over high heat, then cook the pork without stirring or turning it for 4 minutes, until crispy brown and some fat is rendered. Turn and let cook another 1 to 2 minutes. Reduce the heat to low and sauté gently for 4 minutes, then turn the heat off, leaving the pork in the skillet.

2. Meanwhile, in a medium skillet, melt the remaining 1 tablespoon lard over medium heat. Cook the pasilla, poblano, ancho, and chipotle chiles, stirring, until they soften, about 3 minutes.

3. In a mortar, crush the toasted sesame seeds with a pestle and set aside, or grind them in a spice mill. Crush the dried shrimp in the mortar, or run in a food processor until crumbly, and incorporate them into the sesame seeds. Place the shrimp mixture into the skillet with the chiles and add the water. Add the oregano, season with salt, and cook on medium heat until the liquid has evaporated, about 8 minutes.

4. Turn the heat under the pork to high. Once it starts to sizzle, reduce the heat to low, pour the sauce over the pork, and continue to cook over low heat, stirring, until there is no liquid left and the meat is succulent and tender, about 10 minutes. If the sauce is getting too thick, add a few tablespoons of water. Add the sour cream, stir it in well so it is blended, and serve immediately with the corn tortillas.

Chapter 4

HOT
Chicken

Poulet Yassa

4 pounds yellow onions, chopped

1 head garlic, cloves separated, peeled, and chopped

½ cup fresh lemon juice

¼ cup apple cider vinegar

¼ cup prepared mustard

1 ball fermented locust bean paste (*dawadawa*) or 1 tablespoon Maggi Sauce or 1 tablespoon soy sauce

2 fresh green jalapeño chiles, finely chopped

3 fresh habanero chiles or 5 fresh cherry chiles or 15 fresh red finger-type chiles, finely chopped

2 dried chiles de árbol, crumbled

2 teaspoons freshly ground black pepper

1 small bay leaf, crumbled

One 3½-pound chicken, cut into 8 pieces, skin removed if desired

¼ cup peanut oil

¼ small cabbage, cut into small chunks

1 carrot, diced

2 teaspoons salt, or more to your taste

Makes 6 servings

Probably the best known of the West African dishes, *poulet yassa* is a specialty from the Casamance region north of Dakar in Senegal, in which chicken is marinated in onions and lemon juice, then grilled, then stewed with lots of chiles. In Africa, chickens and Guinea fowl are tough and therefore you will see the use of overnight marinades as in this recipe. Here I instruct you to either grill the chicken or bake it in the oven. *Poulet yassa* is good with a cool salad, and the best drinks to accompany it are ginger beer, mint tea, and beer. Authentic recipes use the fermented locust bean, but the Maggi Sauce, readily available in supermarkets, is equally authentic, as this Swiss-produced condiment is quite popular in West Africa. Serve with Rice Pilaf (page 129) or couscous.

1. In a large ceramic or glass bowl, toss together the onions, garlic, lemon juice, vinegar, mustard, fermented locust bean paste, fresh chiles, dried chiles, black pepper, and bay leaf. And the chicken, stirring to coat, and marinate overnight in the refrigerator.

2. Prepare a hot charcoal fire on one side of the grill or preheat a gas grill on medium for 15 minutes. Remove the chicken from the marinade, scraping off the onion pieces and reserving the marinade. Place the chicken on the cool part of the grill, away from the fire, and grill slowly with the hood down until the chicken crispy golden brown and firm to the touch, about 1 hour. Keep checking, because the heat of the grill is quite variable. Alternatively, preheat the oven to 325°F. Place the chicken in a baking dish and bake until golden brown, about 1½ hours. Remove the chicken and set aside, keeping it warm.

3. Meanwhile, place the reserved marinade and onions in a strainer and set over a bowl to separate the liquid from the solid pieces, saving both. In a large casserole or stockpot, heat the oil over medium-high heat, then cook the onions, stirring, until golden, 10 to 12 minutes. Add the reserved liquid marinade to the casserole along with the cabbage and carrot and bring to a boil, then reduce the heat to medium-low, season with the salt, and cook 10 minutes. Add the reserved chicken, cover, and simmer over low heat until the chicken is tender, about 10 minutes. Serve hot.

Kung Pao Chicken

Makes 4 servings

Although this famous Chinese dish, appearing on every Chinese restaurant menu in America, is often assumed to be a Sichuan preparation, it is actually from one of China's least-known provinces. Guizhou is a poor province bordering Sichuan to the northeast. Kung pao (*gong bao*) chicken is a spicy dish made with diced chicken, peanuts, and chile peppers. In kung pao chicken all the ingredients are cut in harmony, and the cubed chicken is complemented by small chunks of scallion. Serve this dish with steamed rice.

1. In a medium bowl, combine 1 tablespoon of the soy sauce, 4½ teaspoons of the cornstarch, and the water and add the chicken, tossing to coat. Marinate for 30 minutes. In another bowl, mix the remaining 2 tablespoons soy sauce, the rice wine, sugar, the remaining 1 teaspoon cornstarch, the salt, and sesame oil and set the sauce aside.

2. In a large wok, heat the vegetable oil over high heat, then cook the chicken until golden, about 1 minute. Remove the chicken with a skimmer and drain. Remove and reserve all but 1½ tablespoons oil from the wok, then let the remaining oil heat over high heat again. Cook the dried chiles until they darken a bit but do not turn black, about 30 seconds, stirring. Remove with a skimmer and set aside.

3. Add 1 tablespoon of the reserved oil to the wok, heat over high heat, and cook the peanuts until they turn golden, about 1 minute. Remove and set aside to cool. Add the remaining 1 tablespoon oil to the wok and let it heat, then cook the ginger, garlic, scallions, and chicken about 1 minute, stir-frying rapidly. Stir in the reserved sauce of soy and rice wine, tossing and stirring until it is well mixed with the other ingredients, about 1 minute, then add the peanuts and stir again. Serve immediately.

3 tablespoons soy sauce

5½ teaspoons cornstarch

1½ tablespoons water

1 pound boneless, skinless chicken breast, cut into ½-inch cubes

1 tablespoon rice wine (mirin) or vermouth

1 tablespoon sugar

½ teaspoon salt

½ teaspoon sesame oil

3 cups vegetable oil, for frying

¾ cup dried chiles de árbol, seeded and halved

½ cup unsalted roasted peanuts

One 1¼-inch-thick slice fresh ginger, peeled and julienned

1 large garlic clove, thinly sliced

2 scallions, cut into ½-inch pieces

Enchiladas Verdes

Makes 6 servings

Enchilada comes from the Spanish verb *enchilar*, which basically means to get chile all over something. An enchilada is something "en-chilied." What this means practically for this recipe is that you will dip the tortilla into the chile sauce. In this "green" version of enchilada, the green color comes from tomatillos and green chiles, while the red version, *enchilada rojo,* is made with tomatoes, red chiles, and chorizo sausage. The one technique that is a little tricky in this preparation is the quick pre-frying of the tortillas. The reason this is done, besides adding some nice flavor, is to make the tortillas softer for rolling and less likely to crack.

1. Bring 6 cups of the water to a boil in a large saucepan and add the tomatillos, 1 small quartered onion, 3 garlic cloves, and 4 serrano chiles. Reduce the heat to medium and simmer until the tomatillos are soft, about 30 minutes. Drain, saving some of the cooking water, and transfer the vegetables to a blender. Add another small quartered onion, 2 garlic cloves, the remaining chiles, and the cilantro to the blender. Blend until smooth, about 2 minutes, adding just enough of the reserved cooking water so the blades of the blender can twirl. Transfer the tomatillo sauce to a skillet or saucepan with ½ teaspoon salt and heat over low heat, covered.

2. Place the chicken breasts in a saucepan and add the remaining 3 cups water, along with three-quarters of the remaining small onion, the remaining ½ teaspoon salt, thyme, the bay leaves, and the remaining 3 garlic cloves. Bring to just below a boil over high heat, and before the water starts bubbling reduce the heat to medium and poach the chicken until firm, about 12 minutes. Let cool in the broth.

3. Meanwhile, finely chop the reserved quarter of onion and set aside. When the chicken is cool enough to handle, remove and discard the bay leaves. Remove the chicken from the saucepan, pull the meat off the bones, discard the skin and bones, and shred the chicken into small pieces. Place the chicken in a skillet or saucepan and keep warm over low heat. Stir in the crème fraîche and the reserved chopped onion. Turn the heat off and cover to keep warm.

9 cups water

1 pound (9 to 12) tomatillos, husked and washed

3 small onions, quartered

8 large garlic cloves, crushed

8 fresh green serrano chiles, stems removed

Leaves from 15 sprigs cilantro

1 teaspoon salt

1¼ pounds bone-in chicken breasts

½ teaspoon dried thyme

2 bay leaves

¼ cup crème fraîche or sour cream

¼ cup vegetable oil, or more if needed

12 corn tortillas

For the Garnish

⅓ cup crumbled Mexican queso añejo, shredded mild white cheddar cheese, shredded Monterey Jack, or crumbled domestic feta

¼ cup crème fraîche or sour cream

2 slices of a medium-size onion, separated into rings

6 radishes, sliced

(continued)

4. In a well-seasoned cast-iron skillet or other heavy skillet, heat the vegetable oil over medium-high heat, then cook the tortillas one at a time until soft, about 3 seconds per side. Remove with tongs and set aside on paper towels to drain. Replenish the oil in the skillet if need be to cook the remaining tortillas.

5. Preheat the oven to 350°F. Pour 1 cup of the tomatillo sauce on a dinner plate and lay a tortilla in the sauce. Fill the center with about 2 tablespoons of the chicken stuffing, then roll up and arrange in a 9 x 13 baking dish. Continue filling and rolling the remaining tortillas. Pour the remaining sauce over the top of the enchiladas. Cover the baking dish with aluminum foil and bake until heated through, about 10 minutes. Remove from the oven, sprinkle with cheese, drizzle with crème fraîche, and garnish with onion rings and radishes. Serve immediately.

Piquant Shredded Chicken
in Creamy Walnut and Chile Sauce

Makes 6 to 8 serving

In the *cocina aymara*, the cuisine of the Aymara Indians in Andean Peru, the potato is the most important food, appearing in every dish they make. This Peruvian dish is called *ají de gallina*, which means "chicken chile" and is a classic dish made in Chiclayo.

1. Place the chicken in a large casserole with the potatoes and cover with water. Bring to just below a boil, then reduce the heat and simmer until the chicken is cooked through and you are able to pull it apart with your fingers, about 2 hours, making sure the water never boils. Remove the chicken from the broth and let cool. Leave the potatoes in the broth for another 20 minutes on low heat. Remove the meat from the chicken bones. Discard the bones and skin, shred the chicken meat with two forks, and set aside. Remove the potatoes, peel, and slice ½ inch thick. Reserve 3 cups of the broth.

2. In a blender, puree the bread, walnuts, and evaporated milk until creamy.

3. In a casserole (you can use the one you poached the chicken in after cleaning it), heat the safflower oil and olive oil over medium-high heat, then cook the onion, garlic, fresh chiles, ground red chile, cayenne pepper, salt, black pepper, and cumin, stirring, until the oil separates and is bubbling, about 3 minutes. Add the bread and walnut cream, bring to a boil, reduce the heat to low, then cook, stirring constantly, until dense, about 5 minutes.

4. Add the shredded chicken, 2 cups of the reserved broth, and the Parmesan cheese and stir over medium heat until it reaches a soft, creamy consistency, about 10 minutes, adding more broth if the sauce is getting too thick. You want to keep the creamy consistency.

5. Arrange the boiled potatoes and white rice next to each other on 6 to 8 individual plates. Spread the shredded chicken on one side, flattening it to cover the plate rather than mounding it. Garnish with the sliced eggs and parsley and serve.

3 pounds bone-in chicken breasts

8 Yukon gold potatoes (about 1½ pounds)

4 slices white bread, crusts removed

1 cup walnut halves

One 12-ounce can evaporated milk

3 tablespoons safflower oil

1 tablespoon extra-virgin olive oil

1 medium-size onion, finely chopped

2 large garlic cloves, crushed

2 fresh red jalapeño chiles, finely chopped

3 tablespoons ground red chile

3 tablespoons cayenne pepper

1 tablespoon salt

2 teaspoons freshly ground black pepper

½ teaspoon ground cumin

1 cup freshly grated Parmesan cheese

2 cups white rice

2 large hard-boiled eggs, sliced, for garnish

Finely chopped fresh parsley leaves, for garnish

Jerk Chicken

For the Jerk Marinade
2 tablespoons ground allspice

2 tablespoons dried thyme

1 tablespoon cayenne pepper

1 tablespoon freshly ground black pepper

1 tablespoon dried sage

1½ teaspoons ground nutmeg

1½ teaspoons ground cinnamon

2 tablespoons salt

6 large garlic cloves

One 1-inch cube fresh ginger

1 tablespoon sugar

½ bunch fresh cilantro, leaves only

¾ cup fresh lime juice

½ cup fresh orange juice

¼ cup soy sauce

¼ cup peanut oil

2 cups chopped scallions

4 fresh Scotch bonnet or fresh habanero chiles, stemmed

For the Chicken
6 pounds mixed bone-in chicken pieces (breasts, thighs, and legs)

3 bay leaves (optional)

Makes 8 to 10 servings

Many travel and food writers recommend that the best place to have jerk in Jamaica is at Boston Bay, near Port Antonio. The secret to jerk—and every jerk man will claim a secret—is a long marinade, slow cooking, and abundant use of the dried berry of the pimento tree, better known as allspice. The branches of the tree are sometimes used as an aromatic wood in the *patas* or grill stands where the jerk is barbecued. Although every part of the chicken can be used for this dish, you must remember to pay close attention to the breasts, as they can dry out if overcooked. Serve with Rice and Peas (page 162) and a green salad.

1. Place all the ingredients for the jerk marinade in a blender and puree until smooth.

2. In a large bowl, toss the chicken pieces with the marinade. Divide the chicken pieces and marinade between two heavy-duty zip-top plastic bags. Seal the bags, pressing out the excess air, and let the chicken marinate in the refrigerator, turning the bags over several times, for at least 6 hours and up to 2 days.

3. Prepare a charcoal fire on one side of the grill or preheat a gas grill on high for 15 minutes, then turn off one set of burners. If using a charcoal grill, toss 3 bay leaves on the coals if desired. Grill the chicken away from the fire, in batches if necessary, and cover, turning every now and then and basting with leftover jerk marinade, until golden brown with bits of blackened skin, about 1½ hours. During the last 30 minutes of cooking keep the chicken breasts skin side up so the meat is farther away from the heat source, and stop basting. If the chicken pieces are blackening too quickly, it means your fire is too hot and you should either keep the cover open, push the coals further away, or lower one of the gas burners. Transfer the jerk chicken to a platter and serve.

Picante de Pollo

Makes 4 to 5 servings

In Bolivia, where this dish is from, it's also known as *sajta*. This preparation is quite definitive of Bolivian cooking and is usually made as part of an even larger feast of *picante mixto*, mixed piquant foods prepared for special occasions and festivities. Some of these other dishes are *picante de lengua*, stuffed potatoes, paste torts, and chile salsas. You can also add coriander seeds and paprika to this and serve it with tomato salad and rice, or *chuño phut*i (dried potato) instead of the potato.

1. Preheat the oven to 400°F. Place the garlic cloves on an ungreased baking sheet and roast until golden, about 8 minutes. Remove and chop finely.

2. In a large casserole, arrange the chicken pieces on the bottom and cover with the onion, tomato, fresh chiles, peas, ground chile, cumin, oregano, salt, black pepper, and oil. Pour the broth over all the ingredients.

3. Bring to a near boil, then reduce the heat to low and simmer, almost completely covered, stirring occasionally and gently, pushing the onion down into the broth and making sure the broth never comes to a boil, until the chicken is nearly falling off the bone, about 2 hours. Remove the chicken and vegetables to a serving platter with the boiled potatoes and spoon some broth over the chicken and potatoes. Sprinkle the chopped parsley on top and serve.

3 large garlic cloves, peeled

One 4-pound chicken, cut into 6 parts

1 large white onion, cut in half and thinly sliced

1 large tomato, peeled, seeded, and finely chopped

4 large fresh red rocoto chiles or 8 fresh red jalapeño chiles, seeded and finely chopped

1 cup fresh or frozen peas or ¼ small cabbage, cut into strips

¼ cup ground ají mirasol or 3 tablespoons cayenne pepper

1 teaspoon ground cumin

1 teaspoon dried oregano

1 tablespoon salt

½ teaspoon freshly ground black pepper

2 tablespoons olive oil or vegetable oil

3 cups chicken broth (homemade or store-bought), dark beer, or water

6 small boiling potatoes, cooked until tender, and peeled

½ cup finely chopped fresh parsley leaves, for garnish

Chicken Cooked in Hell

Makes 4 to 5 servings

No, they don't call it that in Cameroon, a Central African country on the Gulf of Guinea with nearly two hundred different ethnic groups and customs. Cameroonian food is generally very hot, and this recipe is blast-off hot. I developed it from a description by Georges Collinet, a Cameroonian radio presenter and host of National Public Radio's *Afropop Worldwide*. The name of the dish, *folon*, is also the name of the mineral-rich vegetable used in the dish, sometimes known as bitterleaf. Varieties of bitterleaf are eaten throughout Africa. Real *folon* leaf is hard to find in North America, although some African markets in the U.S. might carry it, especially those catering to Nigerian cooks. Bitterleaf has a slightly viscous property, and although some African cookbooks written for the North American market recommend using spinach in its place, collard greens or kale are better choices. The peanut butter used in so much African cooking is not actually "peanut butter" but is the paste of ground peanuts. That might not sound different, but you will get an earthier taste by using organic peanut butter rather than Skippy. Serve this dish with yams, fried plantains, rice, cassava, or all of the above. And as Georges Collinet recommends: "Drink a good, strong beer with your *folon*."

1. In a medium skillet, heat 2 tablespoons of the oil over medium heat, then cook the sliced onion, stirring and turning frequently and separating its rings as it cooks, until golden brown, about 12 minutes. Remove, spread out on a paper towel–lined plate, and set aside.

2. Bring the water to a boil in a large saucepan and boil the collard greens for 30 minutes. Add the chicken and the onion cut into eighths and cook until it returns to a near boil, but not more than 5 minutes. Remove the chicken with a slotted spoon, pat dry with a paper towel, and set aside. Remove the greens with a slotted spoon, cut them into small pieces, and set aside. Reserve 3 cups of the broth. In a medium bowl, mix 1 cup of the broth with the peanut butter so that it becomes more liquid and easier to handle, and set aside.

4 tablespoons peanut oil

3 medium-size onions, 1 thinly sliced, 1 cut into eighths, and 1 chopped

3 quarts water

1 pound fresh collard greens or kale, thick stems removed

3 bone-in chicken breast halves, skin removed

½ pound freshly made peanut butter

3 medium-size tomatoes, cut in half, seeds squeezed out, and grated against the largest holes of a grater

2½ pounds fresh large shrimp with their heads or 1¼ pounds headless shrimp, heads and/or shells removed

2 fresh habanero chiles, finely chopped

Salt and freshly ground black pepper to taste

(continued)

3. In a large skillet, heat the remaining 2 tablespoons peanut oil over medium-high heat, then cook the chicken pieces on all sides until golden brown, about 5 minutes. Remove the chicken, cut each breast in half with a heavy chef's knife, and set aside.

4. Add the chopped onion and the tomatoes to the skillet and cook over medium-high heat, stirring occasionally, until the liquid of the tomatoes has mostly evaporated, about 3 minutes. Add the peanut butter mixture and cook over medium-low heat for 20 minutes, stirring often so that it doesn't stick, and adding ½ cup increments of the remaining reserved broth to keep the sauce creamy. Add the collard greens, shrimp, chiles, and salt and black pepper and stir to blend well. Add the chicken, increase the heat to medium, and cook, partially covered, until the chicken is cooked through and the shrimp are firm and orange-pink, turning occasionally, 15 minutes. If the sauce is bubbling too vigorously, reduce the heat to low. Transfer to a serving platter or individual plates and serve with the fried onions reserved from step 1 scattered on top.

Chicken in Adobo Sauce

Makes 4 to 6 servings

Mexican adobo sauce, so called because it always has vinegar, is a blended sauce of dried chiles soaked in chicken broth and mixed with roasted onions, tomatoes, garlic, and vinegar. It can be used in a variety of dishes, so if there is any left over, save it for something else. In this preparation the chicken pieces swim in an ocean of adobo sauce. When you pull the tender meat off the bone, swirl each bite into the sauce before eating. This dish is nice served with white rice and some warmed corn tortillas.

1. Preheat the oven to 450°F. Place the tomatoes and onion on a baking sheet and roast them until they blacken, about 25 minutes for the tomatoes and 40 minutes for the onion. Remove the skin from the tomatoes. Cut up the tomatoes and onion into smaller pieces and place in a bowl. Reduce the heat of the oven to 350°F.

2. In a bowl, pour the boiling chicken broth over the dried chiles and let soak for 30 minutes, placing a weight such as a smaller bowl on top to keep the chiles submerged. Transfer the chiles and their soaking liquid to a blender and puree at high speed for about 1 minute. Add the roasted tomatoes and onion along with the garlic, vinegar, sugar, coriander, cinnamon, cloves, salt, and black pepper. Blend until it is a thick puree.

3. In a large skillet, melt 1 tablespoon lard over medium heat, then cook the puree, uncovered, for 5 minutes, stirring frequently and lowering the heat a bit if it is splattering. Remove from heat and set aside, covered to keep the adobo sauce warm.

4. Meanwhile, in another large skillet, melt the remaining 3 tablespoons lard over medium heat, then cook the chicken pieces, turning once and scraping up any sticking bits with a spatula, until golden brown, 12 to 14 minutes. Transfer the pieces to a large shallow casserole that you can bring to the table, arranging the chicken pieces in one layer. Pour the reserved adobo sauce over them, making sure all the pieces are coated and covered with sauce. Cover the casserole and bake for 45 minutes. Uncover and bake, basting once, until the chicken can be pulled off the bone with a fork and the sauce is bubbling, about 15 minutes. Serve immediately.

3 medium-size tomatoes (about 1 pound)

1 medium-size onion, cut in half

1 cup chicken broth (homemade or store-bought), boiling

4 dried ancho chiles, seeded, stemmed, and broken into smaller pieces

3 dried guajillo chiles or 4 dried chiles de árbol, seeded, stemmed, and broken into smaller pieces

2 large garlic cloves

1 tablespoon apple cider vinegar

1 teaspoon sugar

½ teaspoon ground coriander

¼ teaspoon ground cinnamon

¼ teaspoon ground cloves

4 teaspoons salt

2 teaspoons freshly ground black pepper

4 tablespoons lard or bacon fat

One 3½-pound chicken, cut into 8 pieces and skin removed

Chicken Kurma

One 1-inch cube fresh ginger, peeled

3 large garlic cloves

¼ cup vegetable oil

1 pound onions, chopped

3 fresh green finger-type chiles or 4 fresh green jalapeño chiles, seeded and finely chopped

2 teaspoons salt

½ teaspoon garam masala made from equal parts cloves, cinnamon, cardamom, and caraway (see box, page 155)

1 teaspoon ground coriander

½ teaspoon ground turmeric

2 pounds bone-in chicken breasts and thighs, skin removed

1 cup Stabilized Yogurt (page 49), whipped until smooth

½ cup water

⅓ cup dried unsweetened shredded coconut

½ teaspoon freshly ground black pepper

1 tablespoon finely chopped fresh cilantro leaves

1 tablespoon finely chopped fresh mint leaves

Makes 4 servings

This dish, from the Indian state of Andhra Pradesh, is very hot, as is most of the food from this region. *Kurma* was originally a Mogul dish and was not so hot spicy as just spicy. Although usually thought of as a northern dish, *kurma* is also made in the south, where a paste from fresh coconut and raw cashews might be used to replace the traditional yogurt or cream used in the north. Serve with plain Rice Pilaf (page 129).

1. Pound the ginger and garlic in a mortar until mushy. Alternatively, use a food processor. In a casserole, heat the oil over medium-high heat, then cook the onions, stirring occasionally, until golden, about 15 minutes. Meanwhile, mix the ginger-garlic paste, the chiles, salt, garam masala, coriander, and turmeric in a bowl, then spread this on the chicken and marinate for 10 minutes.

2. Add the chicken pieces to the onions in the casserole and cook 10 minutes, turning occasionally. Add the yogurt and water and stir well. Cook for 5 minutes, then add the coconut, black pepper, coriander, and mint. Cover, reduce the heat to low, and cook until the chicken is very tender, 15 to 20 minutes. Serve hot.

Sichuan Peppery Chicken

Makes 2 to 4 servings

This brightly colored dish is traditionally made with the meat from chicken legs, but I find that using chicken thighs is much less work and the taste is identical. The dark-fleshed meat becomes golden-purple when it is cooked and it contrasts with the brilliant green or red of the bell pepper. This is a very hot dish and, therefore, you will want to eat it with steamed rice.

Thick pastes made of chiles and beans are called *lajiao jiang*, and they represent a whole class of cooking condiments. You can find them in Chinese groceries and many supermarkets, labeled "hot chile paste with garlic."

1. In a medium-size glass or ceramic bowl, combine the egg white, 1½ teaspoons of the cornstarch, and 1 teaspoon of the soy sauce. Add the chicken, toss to coat, and marinate for 20 to 30 minutes.

2. In a large wok, heat the peanut oil over medium heat to about 250°F. Dip the chicken in the hot oil until it turns color, about 15 seconds, then remove the chicken with a skimmer and set aside. Remove all but 3 tablespoons oil from the wok and raise the heat to medium-high. Cook the fresh chiles, bell pepper, scallion, ginger, and garlic, stirring, until fragrant, about 1 minute. Remove from the wok and set aside with the chicken.

3. Add the chile bean paste and cook until fragrant, about 10 seconds, breaking it up and stirring, then add the dried chiles and Sichuan pepper and stir. Add the reserved chicken and the bell pepper mixture, the rice wine, the remaining 1 teaspoon soy sauce, the sugar, sesame oil, water, vinegar, and the remaining ½ teaspoon cornstarch. Stir several times, then cook over medium-high heat, stirring, until the chicken is cooked through and the bell pepper is softer but still crunchy, about 5 minutes. Serve immediately.

1 egg white, beaten until frothy

2 teaspoons cornstarch

2 teaspoons soy sauce

1 pound boneless, skinless chicken thighs, cut into ½-inch cubes

3 cups peanut oil, for frying

8 fresh red finger-type or fresh red jalapeño chiles, seeded and chopped

1 green or red bell pepper, cut into ¾-inch squares

1 scallion, white part only, finely chopped

1 teaspoon finely chopped fresh ginger

1 large garlic clove, finely chopped

1 tablespoon Sichuan chile bean paste (see headnote)

2 dried chiles de árbol

¼ teaspoon ground Sichuan peppercorns

1½ teaspoons rice wine (mirin) or vermouth

1 teaspoon sugar

1 teaspoon sesame oil

1 teaspoon water

½ teaspoon white vinegar

Chongqing Spicy Chicken

2 pounds chicken wings, cut into 1-inch pieces

1 tablespoon rice wine (mirin) or vermouth

2 teaspoons soy sauce

4 cups peanut oil, for frying

1½ cups rice flour or unbleached all-purpose flour, for dredging

2 large garlic cloves, thinly sliced

One ½-inch cube fresh ginger, peeled and thinly sliced

2 ounces dried chiles de árbol (about 2 cups), halved and seeded

1 tablespoon Sichuan peppercorns

3 scallions, white and light green parts only, cut into thirds

1 teaspoon salt, or more to your taste

½ teaspoon sugar

2 teaspoons sesame oil

Makes 4 servings

It is said that the cuisine of Chongqing, a major industrial city at the junction of the Kialing and Yangtze rivers, is hotter than elsewhere in Sichuan. This dish—simply called chicken with chiles (*la zi ji*) in Chinese—is straightforward in its cooking; the tricky part is the chicken. American supermarkets don't sell the wings cut up the way you need them for this preparation. So you will have to buy chicken wings, preferably from a quite young bird, and cut each wing into four to five pieces. When I tried this dish at the Sam Luk Restaurant in San Francisco it had crunchy golden chicken pieces so tender that you could eat the bones as well. I've not been able to reproduce that in my home kitchen because I don't have access to young chickens, but you can get the tastes exactly right by buying supermarket chicken wings and following this recipe. Although this recipe uses an impossible amount of chiles, diners usually pick out the chicken with their chopsticks and not the chiles. Even so, the dish can only be described as incendiary.

1. Toss the chicken in a large glass or ceramic bowl with the rice wine and soy sauce and marinate for 30 minutes.

2. In a large wok, heat the peanut oil to 300°F over medium heat. Drain the chicken and toss with the flour until lightly coated, shaking off any excess flour in a colander. Cook the chicken in 3 batches until golden brown and a little crispy, 7 to 8 minutes. Remove each batch with a skimmer and set aside.

3. Remove all but 3 tablespoons peanut oil from the wok and heat over medium heat. Add the garlic and ginger and cook, stirring, until they start to turn color, about 20 seconds. Add the chiles and Sichuan peppercorns and cook 20 seconds, stirring. Remove the wok from the heat if the chiles look like they are turning black. Return the chicken to the wok, add the scallions, and stir. Season with salt and sugar, stir, and toss until the chicken is well coated. Remove from the heat and stir in the sesame oil. Serve immediately.

Chapter 5

SEAFOOD with a Kick

Spicy Shrimp
with Ají Sauce

4 pounds fresh large shrimp with their heads or 2 pounds headless shrimp, heads and/or shells removed

3 tablespoons unsalted butter

4 tablespoons extra-virgin olive oil

2 medium-size white onions, finely chopped

4 large garlic cloves, mashed in a mortar with 1 teaspoon salt

2 medium-size tomatoes, peeled, seeded, and chopped

1 tablespoon finely chopped fresh tarragon leaves

1 teaspoon dried thyme

½ cup dry white wine

¼ cup Yellow Chile Sauce (*Ají*; opposite)

1 teaspoon salt, or more to your taste

1 teaspoon freshly ground white pepper

4 slices white bread, crusts removed and soaked in half-and-half or milk

¼ cup water

½ pound walnuts, coarsely chopped

2¾ cups heavy cream

1 tablespoon flour mixed with 1 tablespoon water (optional)

Makes 6 servings

This famous and fabulous Peruvian dish is called *picante de camarones*, which basically means "hot shrimp." It's an over-the-top dish that is rich and satisfying. The *ají* (pronounced ah-hee) sauce used in this dish is made with the fresh yellow chiles called *ají amarillo fresco* in Peru. As these are unlikely to be found in your supermarket, you can replace them with the yellow chile sauce. If you are using fresh shrimp and any of them have their eggs attached, remove the coral and add it to the skillet in step 2 at the same time you add the walnuts. Peruvians always serve this with boiled yellow potatoes (you can use Yukon gold), wedges of hard-boiled egg for garnish, and steamed rice to cut through the heat.

1. Bring a large pot of abundantly salted water to a boil over high heat, then plunge the shrimp in. Cook them until they turn orange-red and are firm, about 3 minutes. Drain and set aside.

2. In a large skillet or casserole, melt the butter with 1 tablespoon of the olive oil over medium-high heat, then cook the onions, garlic, and tomatoes, stirring, until the onions are soft, about 6 minutes. Add the remaining 3 tablespoons olive oil, the tarragon, thyme, wine, and yellow chile sauce. Season with 1 teaspoon salt and ½ teaspoon white pepper and bring to a boil. Cook until most of the wine has evaporated, about 3 minutes, then reduce the heat to low and simmer until a little denser, about 3 minutes, stirring occasionally. Squeeze the liquid out of the bread and add the soaked bread to the skillet along with the water, walnuts, and cream and cook, stirring occasionally and making sure the sauce does not boil, until velvety and saucy, about 30 minutes. If a thicker sauce is desired, add the flour and water mixture to the sauce, while stirring.

3. Add the reserved shrimp, add more salt if desired and the remaining ½ teaspoon white pepper, and heat the shrimp for about 5 minutes. Serve immediately.

Yellow Chile Sauce (*Ají*)

Makes about 1¼ cups

A bowl of *ají* appears on every table in Bolivia and Peru as a condiment to soups, stews, ceviches, and nearly everything else. It is made with fresh yellow chiles called *ají amarillo fresco*. In your supermarket, look for yellow chiles, banana chiles, Hungarian wax chiles, or yellow *güero* chiles. Look for yellow chiles about three inches long and one inch wide at the stem. You could also make this with red or green chiles. The red finger-type chiles are about four inches long and a half inch wide at the stem and the green chiles are your typical large jalapeño chiles. In this recipe, I've adapted the chiles used to create something akin to South American chiles. You can put this sauce on the table whenever you are having a Peruvian or Bolivian dinner.

Place the chiles, olive oil, water, and salt in a blender and process until smooth, adding a little more water if necessary to make it puree. Scrape down the sides. Store in the refrigerator for 1 week or freeze indefinitely.

20 fresh yellow chiles or 18 fresh red finger-type chiles or 12 large fresh green jalapeño chiles, seeded and coarsely chopped

1 fresh habanero chile, seeded and chopped

1 tablespoon extra-virgin olive oil

¼ cup water, plus more if needed

2 teaspoons salt

Shredded Shrimp and Serrano Chile Tacos

Makes 4 servings

This dish is from the Mexican state of Sinaloa where it is called *tacos de machaca de camarón*. It's a fun recipe because you finely chop the shrimp, spice it dramatically with chiles, and then roll it into tortillas. Sprinkle some of the garnish inside the taco before you wrap it up. Because the shrimp is very hot, the mild garnishes both temper the heat and provide a delightful counter to the chiles. This recipe is adapted from one by Marilu Monem de Lopez.

In a large skillet, heat the corn oil and butter over medium heat, then add the onion and cook, stirring occasionally, until the onion is golden, about 10 minutes. Add the serrano and poblano chiles, tomatoes, and oregano and simmer, stirring occasionally, until the sauce is thick, about 25 minutes. Add the shrimp, reduce the heat to low, and simmer, stirring occasionally, until very thick, with no remaining liquid, about 25 minutes. Season with salt and black pepper. Transfer to a serving platter and serve with the tortillas and garnishes.

3 tablespoons corn oil

3 tablespoons unsalted butter

1 very large white onion, finely chopped

6 fresh green serrano chiles, finely chopped

1 fresh green poblano chile, roasted, peeled, seeded, and finely chopped

1¾ pounds tomatoes, cut in half, seeds squeezed out, and grated against the largest holes of a grater

2 teaspoons dried oregano

2 pounds fresh medium-size shrimp with their heads or 1 pound headless shrimp, heads and/or shells removed, meat finely chopped or ground in a food processor until shredded

Salt and freshly ground black pepper to taste

4 large flour tortillas, warmed

For Garnish (Choose 1 or 2)

Shredded iceberg lettuce

Chopped ripe tomatoes

Chopped scallions

Chopped fresh cilantro leaves

Shredded cabbage

Shrimp Creole

3 pounds fresh jumbo shrimp with their heads or 1½ pounds headless jumbo shrimp, heads and/or shells removed and reserved

2 tablespoons fresh lime juice

2 teaspoons salt, or more to your taste

1 teaspoon freshly ground black pepper, or more to your taste

3 tablespoons unsalted butter

1 medium-size onion, finely chopped

12 scallions, white and light green parts only, finely chopped

4 shallots, finely chopped

6 large garlic cloves, finely chopped

2 fresh Scotch bonnet chiles or fresh habanero chiles, seeded and finely chopped

One ½-inch cube fresh ginger, peeled and finely chopped

1½ teaspoons curry powder

2¼ pounds ripe tomatoes, peeled, seeded, and chopped

1 cup finely chopped fresh parsley leaves

¼ cup finely chopped fresh cilantro leaves

1 teaspoon fresh thyme leaves, finely chopped

1 bay leaf

⅓ cup dark rum

2 tablespoons tomato paste

Makes 6 servings

Recipes of every kind abound for this well-known Louisiana dish. But there are certain ingredients that always appear in shrimp Creole, namely shrimp, tomatoes, onions, and chiles. Some cooks also add Tabasco or Worcestershire sauce. Creole cooking was born in New Orleans in the early eighteenth century as a mixture of three basic traditions: French, Spanish, and Afro-Caribbean. There were other influences, including Sicilian, Native American, and Mexican. As Paul Prudhomme pointed out, Creole cooking is a sophisticated city cooking that exists only in the home today, as restaurants have blended the distinction between Creole and Cajun. This recipe is adapted from an unattributed source in a New Orleans promotion on a travel website, but I feel that it must come from a very good cook because it evidences not only a good taste but a sophisticated balance of flavors. The use of Scotch bonnet chiles in this recipe, rather than the more common use of jalapeño or serrano, points to an early introduction by Afro-Caribbean cooks. This dish is traditionally eaten with rice.

1. Put the shrimp heads and/or shells in a saucepan and cover with water. Bring to a boil over high heat, reduce the heat to low, and simmer until needed.

2. Place the shrimp in a large bowl and pour the lime juice over them. Season with salt and black pepper and set aside until needed.

3. In a large skillet, melt the butter over medium heat, then cook the onion, scallions, shallots, 5 of the garlic cloves, the chiles, ginger, and curry powder until the mixture is soft and yellow, about 5 minutes. Stir in the tomatoes, ½ cup of the parsley, the cilantro, thyme, and bay leaf. Increase the heat to high and cook, stirring, for 1 minute. Stir in the rum and bring to a boil.

4. Strain the shrimp broth. Add 1 cup of the shrimp broth and the tomato paste to the skillet, reserving the rest for another use. Reduce the heat to medium and simmer, stirring frequently, until thickened, about 20 minutes.

5. Add the shrimp to the skillet, reduce the heat to low, and stir to coat the shrimp with the sauce. Simmer, turning occasionally, until the shrimp are curled and orange-pink, about 5 minutes. Stir in the remaining garlic and cook 1 minute. Sprinkle with the remaining ½ cup parsley and cook 1 minute. Serve immediately.

Fresh Shrimp

Fresh shrimp as described in my recipes means never-having-been frozen shrimp. Fresh shrimp is nearly impossible to find and I'm able to track it down only once a year. Nearly all commercial shrimp is flash-frozen, and what you are eating when you buy shrimp at the supermarket or fish store is defrosted shrimp. Is there really such a difference? Yes, there is. I know people brought up on fresh shrimp who refuse to eat frozen shrimp because you might as well eat imitation crabmeat. Fresh shrimp are always sold with heads on. If you ever encounter them, buy ten pounds and make a bunch of shrimp recipes.

Catfish Stew

¾ cup (1½ sticks) unsalted butter

1 cup finely chopped red bell peppers

⅔ cup finely chopped green bell peppers

½ cup finely chopped celery

5 scallions, trimmed of outer green portions and finely chopped

2 fresh green finger-type chiles or 3 fresh green jalapeño chiles, seeded and finely chopped

2 tablespoons finely chopped fresh cilantro leaves

¼ cup Cliff's Cajun Seasoning (opposite)

½ cup dry white wine

2 cups shrimp broth (homemade or store-bought)

2 cups heavy cream

Zest from ½ orange, grated

1 bay leaf

1½ pounds catfish fillets, cut into 1-inch cubes

6 slices Italian or French bread, lightly toasted

Makes 6 servings

When you're in Louisiana you hear about crawfish constantly. But the Cajuns do enjoy other seafood, including catfish. This rich stew is made with catfish in Bayou country, but you could use any firm-fleshed fish such as mahimahi, monkfish, opah, grouper, striped bass, or shark. Serve it with rice, dumplings, or cornbread.

1. In a large casserole or stockpot, melt ½ cup (1 stick) of the butter over medium-high heat. When the bubbles subside, add the red bell pepper, green bell pepper, celery, scallions, chiles, and cilantro. Add Cliff's cajun seasoning and cook, stirring frequently, for 8 minutes.

2. Pour in the wine and let it cook for 3 minutes, stirring frequently. Add 1 cup of the shrimp broth and 1 cup of the heavy cream. Add the orange zest and bay leaf. Reduce the heat to medium and cook for 20 minutes until the liquid has thickened.

3. Pour in the remaining 1 cup shrimp broth and 1 cup heavy cream. Cook for 30 minutes more. Add the catfish and cook until firm, about 15 minutes. Remove and discard the bay leaf. Serve immediately in soup bowls with toast on the side for dipping into the stew.

Cliff's Cajun Seasoning

Makes 6 tablespoons

There's a million so-called Cajun spice blends. Commercially, the two most widely available are Tony Chachere's Creole Seasoning and Paul Prudhomme's Magic Seasoning blends. This recipe is similar to those.

Place all the ingredients in a spice mill and run until ground. Alternatively, mix all the ingredients together in a bowl. Store in a jar and keep with your other spices.

2 tablespoon salt

2 teaspoon freshly ground black pepper

2 teaspoon freshly ground white pepper

2 teaspoon garlic powder

1 teaspoon cayenne pepper

1 teaspoon paprika

1 teaspoon onion powder

½ teaspoon ground coriander

½ teaspoon ground cumin

¼ teaspoon dried basil

¼ teaspoon dried oregano

¼ teaspoon dried thyme

Hot Crab Dip

8 ounces cream cheese

½ cup (1 stick) unsalted butter

1 pound crabmeat, picked over

1 small onion, finely chopped

2 teaspoons Tabasco sauce

2 teaspoons garlic powder

2 teaspoons cayenne pepper

2 teaspoons salt

2 teaspoons freshly ground
    white pepper

Makes 3 cups

Now here's a dip that will keep a party hopping and hot. You can tell your guests that this is a typical Cajun party dip served at everything from beer-swilling shindigs to family gatherings. The recipe is adapted from one by Suzanne LeMaire and it is temperature-hot *and* chile-hot. You can use crackers or tart shells for scooping up the dip. The Frito's corn chips called Scoops that are made especially for dipping are a splurge, but celery or carrot sticks are equally nice.

In a double boiler over medium-high heat, melt the cream cheese and butter, stirring. Once the mixture has become homogeneous, reduce the heat to medium-low, add the crabmeat, onion, Tabasco, garlic powder, cayenne pepper, salt, and white pepper, and stir until the dip is heated through, about 5 minutes. Add additional seasoning to your taste and serve hot.

Goan Fish Curry

Makes 4 servings

There are many dishes described as "fish curry" from Goa, from Bengal, and elsewhere and no one is the same. This preparation from Goa is unique because you make the coconut milk by spicing the coconut, then putting the spiced coconut shavings in a blender. Goan food is also very, very hot, of that there is no doubt. Halibut has a rather heavy bone and therefore 2 pounds will serve four people. This dish can also be made with shrimp.

1. Wash the fish, then pat dry with paper towels and place in a bowl. Toss with the onion, green chiles, and salt. Set aside in the refrigerator.

2. In a blender, combine the coconut, garlic, ginger, dried chiles, coriander seeds, cumin seeds, peppercorns, turmeric, and 3 cups of the water. Blend this mixture in batches if necessary, until smooth.

3. Pour the liquid through a strainer into a bowl, squeezing as much liquid as you can out of the coconut mixture with the back of a wooden spoon. Put the solids back into the blender with the remaining ½ cup water and blend again for 1 minute. Strain the liquid again, pressing as much liquid out as you can.

4. Pour the strained coconut milk into a deep pan or casserole. Cook over medium heat, stirring occasionally until it thickens, about 30 minutes. Whisk in the tamarind paste and cook for 1 or 2 minutes while it softens. Add the fish mixture and cook, turning once or twice, until it begins to flake, about 12 minutes. If the sauce is evaporating before the fish is fully cooked, cover and add a little water. Serve immediately.

4 halibut or cod steaks (about 2 pounds)

1 medium-size onion, thinly sliced

4 fresh green finger-type chiles or 5 fresh green jalapeño chiles, seeded and julienned lengthwise

Salt to taste

2 cups tightly packed grated fresh coconut or dried unsweetened shredded coconut

6 large garlic cloves

One ½-inch cube fresh ginger, peeled

8 dried chiles de árbol, seeded

1 tablespoon coriander seeds

1½ teaspoons cumin seeds

4 black peppercorns

½ teaspoon ground turmeric

3½ cups warm water

2 tablespoons tamarind paste

Swordfish in the "Sauce That Dances"

Makes 4 to 6 servings

In Algeria, this dish is called *kalb al-bahr shatitha*. The first part of this name, *kalb al-bahr*, is the Arabic name for dogfish, an unfortunate name for a delicious small shark also known as Cape shark on the eastern U.S. coast. Any firm-fleshed fish such as another kind of shark or swordfish works very well here. I use swordfish because it's easy to get, if expensive. The second part of the Algerian name means literally the "sauce that dances," meaning that it is very piquant. The spicy-hot food "dances" in your mouth, and it also "dances" in the skillet, since it is cooked quickly. The word *shatitha* derives from *shatta*, a variety of chile. This is a spectacular dish with swordfish and wonderful served with fettuccine.

In a large skillet or stovetop earthenware tagine with a cover, mix together the olive oil, garlic, chile, water, cayenne pepper, paprika, 1 teaspoon salt, cumin, coriander, black pepper, harissa, bay leaf, and thyme. Bring to just boiling over high heat, then reduce the heat to low, add the fish and tomatoes, salt lightly, cover, and cook until the fish is firm, about 25 minutes. Serve immediately.

13 tablespoons extra-virgin olive oil

1 large garlic clove, finely chopped

1 fresh green finger-type chile or 2 fresh green jalapeño chiles, seeded and finely chopped

3 tablespoons water

2 teaspoons cayenne pepper

1 teaspoon hot paprika

1 teaspoon salt, plus more to taste

1 teaspoon ground cumin

1 teaspoon ground coriander

1 teaspoon freshly ground black pepper

1 teaspoon Harissa (page 25)

1 bay leaf, finely crumbled

½ teaspoon dried thyme

4 to 6 swordfish steaks (about 1¾ pounds)

1 pound ripe tomatoes, peeled, seeded, and chopped

Bengali Fish Stew

1 teaspoon hot paprika

½ teaspoon ground turmeric

Salt to taste

1¼ pounds sea bass, cod, or halibut steaks, cut into 2-inch cubes

3 tablespoons mustard oil or vegetable oil

3 large onions, finely chopped

4 large garlic cloves, crushed

4 fresh green finger-type chiles or 6 green jalapeño chiles, seeded and finely chopped

¼ teaspoon ground cumin

¼ teaspoon mustard seeds

⅛ teaspoon ground cinnamon

⅛ teaspoon ground cloves

⅛ teaspoon ground cardamom

1½ pounds ripe tomatoes, cut in half, seeds squeezed out, and grated against the largest holes of a grater

1 tablespoon chopped fresh cilantro leaves

¼ cup water

½ cup whole plain yogurt or Stabilized Yogurt (page 49)

Makes 4 servings

West Bengal is part of India and East Bengal is Bangladesh. In both Bengals fish is extremely popular and in both Bengals the most famous dishes are fish dishes. Although there are a variety of styles of cooking fish in Bengal, the two main ones are cooking fish in spices and cooking fish in yogurt. In West Bengal mustard oil is used prominently as a cooking fat, while in Bangladesh coconut oil is more common. Two of the most popular fish used in this preparation, called *machher jhol*, are *rohu* and pomfret. Many cooks also add two vegetables to the stew, such as potatoes and eggplants in small dice. Serve with rice.

1. Mix the paprika, ¼ teaspoon of the turmeric, and the salt on a plate. Dredge the fish on both sides in the mixture. In a large skillet, heat the oil over medium-high heat and brown the fish on both sides, about 3 minutes in all, turning once. Remove and set aside.

2. Add the onions and garlic to the skillet and cook, stirring frequently, until soft and yellow, about 15 minutes. Add the chiles, cumin, mustard seeds, cinnamon, cloves, cardamom, and the remaining ¼ teaspoon turmeric. Cook for 2 minutes, stirring, then add the tomatoes, cilantro, and water. Reduce the heat to low and cook until the sauce is dense, about 15 minutes. Add the yogurt and salt to taste and stir to blend. Return the fish to the skillet, cover, and simmer until the fish flakes, about 10 minutes. Make sure that the broth never becomes too hot or the yogurt might separate, unless you are using stabilized yogurt. Serve immediately.

Andouille Sausage, Shrimp, and Oyster Gumbo

Makes 4 servings

It's hard to say how gumbo was invented, although its connection to Africa is not in doubt. One legend is that it came about when okra was introduced to Mobile, Alabama, in 1704 by twenty-five French mademoiselles known as the "Cassette girls," who arrived in search of husbands. They came by way of the West Indies, where they had acquired okra from African slaves who called the plant gumbo and used it in stews also called gumbo. Today, a gumbo does not have to contain okra. The most popular ingredients in gumbo are andouille sausage, shrimp, oysters, crab, duck, chicken, and, among more rural cooks, alligator, squirrel, venison, and nutria. I'm wild about gumbos, especially when they mix meats with seafood, as in this recipe. Serve over rice.

1. In a large skillet, heat the oil over medium heat and brown the sausage, about 8 minutes. Transfer the sausage to a platter with a slotted spoon and pour off all but 2 tablespoons of fat. Make a roux by adding the flour and stirring almost constantly with a whisk or wooden spoon for about 45 minutes or until dark golden brown, adjusting the heat downward if it is cooking too fast.

2. Add the red and green bell peppers and the onion. Reduce the heat to low and cook, stirring occasionally, until the vegetables are soft, 6 to 10 minutes. Add a few tablespoons of water and scrape up any residue on the bottom of the pan.

3. In a saucepan, bring the 6 cups water to a boil with the salt and bay leaf. Drop the shrimp into the boiling water and boil for 2 minutes. Remove the shrimp with a slotted ladle and store in the refrigerator. Reduce the heat to low. Peel the shrimp, throwing the heads and shells back into the simmering water, and let the broth simmer for 15 minutes

4. Strain the shrimp broth, discarding the heads, shells, and bay leaf. Pour the broth into a clean pot and bring to a boil over high heat. Stir in the roux mixture, the sausage, oyster liquid, tomatoes, shallots, cayenne pepper, thyme, oregano, black pepper, and Tabasco sauce and simmer for 2 hours over low heat, stirring occasionally.

5. Stir in the shrimp, oysters, and cilantro and cook until the shrimp are orange and the edges of the oysters have curled up, 2 to 3 minutes. Serve immediately.

2 tablespoons vegetable oil

1 pound smoked andouille sausage, sliced

¼ cup unbleached all-purpose flour

1 small red bell pepper, chopped

1 small green bell pepper, chopped

1 medium-size onion, thinly sliced

6 cups water, plus a few tablespoons

2 tablespoons salt

1 bay leaf

20 ounces fresh shrimp with their heads or 10 ounces headless shrimp, shells left on

24 oysters, shucked, liquid reserved

One 14-ounce can Italian plum tomatoes with their liquid

½ cup sliced shallots

2 teaspoons cayenne pepper

½ teaspoon dried thyme

½ teaspoon dried oregano

Freshly ground black pepper to taste

½ teaspoon Tabasco sauce

2 tablespoons finely chopped fresh cilantro leaves

Grilled Shrimp
with Piri-Piri Sauce

Makes 4 servings

This fantastically hot shrimp dish from Mozambique is made with *piri-piri*, a very hot red chile sauce. This preparation of grilled shrimp is still known there by its Portuguese name, *camarão grelhado piripiri*. Some people think that the Ethiopian spice mix berbere is a corruption of *piri-piri*. *Piri-piri's* home is truly Mozambique where they eat it in what some would call excess. Some Mozambiquan versions use only lemon juice. Versions from West Africa use tomatoes and sometimes red wine. The shrimp can also be poached in water and lemon juice, but I think grilled is too spectacular to pass up. Grilled shrimp with fiery sauces are popular in coastal Africa. The colossal shrimp called for in this recipe have about twelve headless shrimp to a pound. Buy the largest shrimp available.

1. Place the peanut oil, fresh red chiles, habanero chiles, garlic, lemon juice, paprika, ground chile, and salt in a blender and blend until smooth. Transfer to a bowl, mix the shrimp into the sauce, and leave to marinate in the refrigerator for 4 to 6 hours.

2. Prepare a hot charcoal fire or preheat a gas grill on high for 15 minutes. In a small bowl, stir the butter and lemon juice together. Skewer the shrimp in two places lengthwise, 4 shrimp per skewer, making sure they don't touch each other. Grill 3 inches from the fire, turning once, until slightly blackened, firm, and orange-pink, 4 to 8 minutes in all. Remove from the grill, arrange on a serving platter, and pour the lemon butter over the shrimp. Serve hot.

¾ cup peanut oil

5 fresh red finger-type chiles or 7 red jalapeño chiles or 4 red cherry or cascabel chiles, stems and seeds removed, roughly chopped

2 fresh habanero chiles, stemmed, seeded, and roughly chopped

4 large garlic cloves, roughly chopped

3 tablespoons fresh lemon juice

1 tablespoon hot paprika

2 tablespoons ground red chile or cayenne pepper

2 teaspoons salt

4 pounds fresh colossal shrimp, heads left on and shells removed, or 2 pounds headless shrimp, shells removed

6 tablespoons unsalted butter, melted

3 tablespoons fresh lemon juice

Six 10-inch long wooden skewers

Stir-Fried Catfish Dry Curry
with Chiles and Ginger

3 tablespoons peanut oil or vegetable oil

1 pound catfish fillets or mixed firm-fleshed fish, cut into small cubes

15 fresh green Thai chiles, stemmed and halved lengthwise, or 6 fresh green serrano chiles, stemmed and quartered lengthwise

2 shallots, thinly sliced

1½ tablespoons finely chopped fresh ginger

4 large garlic cloves, finely chopped

1 tablespoon green peppercorns

1 teaspoon freshly ground white pepper

2 tablespoons coarsely chopped fresh basil or cilantro leaves

Makes 4 servings

Pad cha is a "dry" curry, which means that no broth is used. This dish can be made with small cubes of fried catfish or it can be made with mixed fish, such as swordfish, yellowtail, and mahimahi. The fish is cooked quickly first and then the other ingredients are stir-fried before the fish returns to the wok to finish cooking. Garnished with either Thai basil or cilantro, it is excellent with steamed rice.

1. In a large wok, heat the oil over high heat and, once it is smoking, cook the fish (in 2 batches if your wok is small) until crispy, 3 to 4 minutes. Remove the fish from the oil with a slotted spoon and set aside, keeping it warm.

2. Add the chiles, shallots, ginger, garlic, peppercorns, and white pepper to the wok and cook until softened and any moisture has evaporated, 4 to 5 minutes. Add the herbs, cook 1 more minute, and pour the curry over the reserved fish. Serve immediately.

Coconut Shrimp

Makes 6 servings

Variations of coconut shrimp appear in Jamaica and other Caribbean islands, especially in tourist restaurants, and in the Florida Keys and in other areas of Florida. It also appears in several guises as a southern dish from New Orleans to Tennessee to Georgia. This is the Jamaican version, and it is very hot and nutty in taste. This recipe is adapted from Lucinda Scala Quinn's *Jamaican Cooking* (Macmillan, 1997) and from a version that I had in a restaurant in Key Largo.

1. Put the lime juice, 1 tablespoon of the oil, the honey, rum, chile, and ½ teaspoon salt in a blender and blend until smooth. Transfer the dipping sauce to a small serving bowl.

2. In a medium bowl, combine the egg whites, Worcestershire sauce, and the remaining ½ teaspoon salt and beat until it is very frothy but not completely stiff. Spread the coconut on a plate. Dip each shrimp in the egg white mixture, then roll in the coconut and transfer to a platter. Refrigerate the shrimp for 30 minutes.

3. In a large skillet, heat the remaining 1 cup oil over high heat until it is smoking, then cook the shrimp until golden brown on one side, about 1 minute, making sure they don't touch each other in the skillet. You may need to cook in batches. Turn them over one at a time, quickly, and cook until the other side is golden brown, 1 to 1½ minutes. Remove and drain on a paper towel–lined platter. Serve the shrimp with the dipping sauce.

Juice of 1 lime

1 cup plus 1 tablespoon vegetable oil

1 tablespoon orange blossom honey

1 tablespoon dark rum

1 fresh Scotch bonnet chile or fresh habanero chile, finely chopped

1 teaspoon salt, or more to your taste

2 large egg whites

½ teaspoon Worcestershire sauce

1½ cups dried unsweetened shredded coconut

2 pounds fresh medium-size shrimp with their heads or 1 pound defrosted headless medium-size shrimp, heads and/or shells removed

Mahimahi
with Green Chile and Cilantro Cream Sauce

6 mahimahi steaks
(about 2 pounds)

Juice of 1 lime

Salt and freshly ground black
pepper to taste

3 green bell peppers

4 fresh green finger-type chiles
or 6 green serrano chiles

1 cup crème fraîche

3 tablespoons finely chopped
fresh cilantro leaves

1 tablespoon extra-virgin olive oil

Makes 6 servings

This Mexican dish from the Pacific coast is called *pescado en salsa verde*, fish in green sauce. You can use just about any kind of firm-fleshed fish, but mahimahi (also called dolphinfish) is both perfect and authentic. The dish appears to be very hot, but the crème fraîche moderates the heat successfully. Serve with Skillet-Fried Potatoes with Green Chiles (page 168) or rice and tortillas.

1. Place the fish steaks in a glass or ceramic baking dish, add the lime juice and salt and black pepper, and marinate for 2 hours in the refrigerator.

2. Preheat the oven to 425°F. Place the bell peppers and chiles in a baking dish and roast until the skin blisters black, 30 to 40 minutes. The chiles will probably be done first, so remove them when they're ready. When the peppers and chiles are cool enough to handle, peel them and remove their stems and the bell pepper seeds. Place in a blender with the crème fraîche and cilantro and blend until smooth, about 2 minutes. Add salt and black pepper if desired.

3. In a large skillet, heat the olive oil over high heat, then brown the fish steaks on both sides, turning with a spatula, about 3 minutes in all. Reduce the heat to low, add the sauce from the blender, pushing the fish steaks around a bit and spooning some sauce over them, cover, and simmer until cooked through, about 18 minutes. Serve immediately.

Shrimp Hash in Coconut Cream

1½ cups coconut milk (see page 21)

¼ teaspoon salt

6 ounces uncooked shelled and deheaded shrimp, very finely chopped

2 tablespoons palm sugar or granulated sugar

1 tablespoon tamarind paste dissolved in 1 tablespoon hot water

1 tablespoon Thai fish sauce

½ small green mango, julienned

4 shallots, thinly sliced

8 fresh green finger-type chiles or 10 green jalapeño chiles, julienned lengthwise in ½-inch lengths

2 tablespoons coarsely chopped fresh cilantro leaves

Makes 4 to 6 servings

This intriguing dish, called *lon gung*, is adapted from a recipe published in 1926 and ascribed to Mom Luang Yingdin Clamarakpitjan, which was made popular by David Thompson, author of several important books on Thai food. The final dish should be creamy, slightly sour, salty, a little sweet, and fiery hot. This is a rich dish that is best served as a main course with some rice.

In a saucepan, bring the coconut milk and salt to a boil, then add the shrimp and cook, stirring constantly to break up the clumped shrimp pieces, until firm and orange, about 3 minutes. Add the sugar, tamarind water, fish sauce, mango, shallots, and chiles and cook until boiling again, about 3 minutes. Sprinkle with cilantro and serve.

Shrimp in Mina Sauce

Makes 8 appetizer servings or 4 main-course servings

This dish from Togo, a small, narrow country in West Africa, is a very hot one that uses both dried and fresh shrimp in a sauce called *mina* sauce. *Mina* is the name of one of the two major African languages spoken in the southern part of Togo. This appetizer or snack is usually served with *fufu*, a starch dish made with fermented cassava flour.

1. In a large skillet or casserole, heat the oil over low heat for 10 minutes, then add the tomatoes, onions, and chiles and cook, stirring occasionally, until the sauce is slightly dense, 1 to 1½ hours, depending on how liquidy your tomatoes were.

2. Add the dried shrimp, salt, and ginger and cook, stirring, for 10 minutes. Add the fresh shrimp and cook, stirring and turning, until they are firm and pink-orange, 5 to 8 minutes.

½ cup peanut oil or ¼ cup red palm oil and ¼ cup peanut oil

2¼ pounds ripe tomatoes, cut in half, seeds squeezed out, and grated against the largest holes of a grater

2 medium-size onions, finely chopped

3 habanero chiles, finely chopped

1 ounce dried whole shrimp or 6 ounces smoked shrimp or one 3-ounce can smoked mussels or one 3-ounce can smoked oysters

2 teaspoons salt, or more to your taste

1 teaspoon ground ginger

4 pounds fresh shrimp with their heads or 2 pounds headless large shrimp, heads and/or shells removed

Chapter 6

VOLATILE
Vegetables

Callaloo

2 pounds callaloo, Swiss chard or spinach, heavy stems removed, rinsed well, and chopped

1 large onion, finely chopped

5 large garlic cloves, 3 finely chopped and 2 lightly crushed

2 ounces salt pork, chopped

1½ cups coconut milk (see page 21)

5 cups water

½ pound fresh crabmeat, picked over

½ pound small okra, trimmed

1 fresh Scotch bonnet chile or fresh habanero chile, seeded and finely chopped

Salt and freshly ground black pepper to taste

Makes 6 servings

Callaloo, also spelled *callalu*, is the name of a Caribbean vegetable stew and also the name for a number of plants used in this and other dishes in Jamaica and Trinidad. The vegetable called callaloo used in this stew is the leaves from Indian kale (also called *malanga* or *yautia*) or Chinese spinach (also called Tahitian taro, tannier spinach, or *belembe*) or taro (also called *dasheen, tannia,* or *cocoyam*). To make matters a little more complicated, the roots of all these plants are known by different names than the leaves. Another name for this dish is "run down" or "pepperpot," and it can also be made with the addition of tomatoes, potatoes, chayote, scallions, and bell pepper. Apparently it is similar to the one made on Tobago, according to Jessica Harris, author of *Sky Juice and Flying Fish: Traditional Caribbean Cooking* (Simon & Schuster, 1991), who also tells us that *cassareep*, a condiment prepared from cassava juice, salt, and pepper, is used in the preparation of pepperpot in Guyana, Trinidad, and Grenada, an inheritance from the aboriginal Arawaks. It may be possible to find fresh callaloo in Caribbean markets; when I cannot locate it, I find Swiss chard to be an excellent substitute.

Put the greens, onion, garlic, salt pork, coconut milk, and water in a large stockpot. Bring to a gentle boil over medium heat. When the salt pork is tender, after about 20 minutes, add the crabmeat, okra, chile, salt, and black pepper and cook until the okra are soft and the stew is bubbling gently, about 12 minutes. Serve hot.

Spicy Cabbage in Coconut Milk

Makes 4 servings as a main course or 6 servings as a side dish

This spicy Indonesian cabbage dish is called *sayur kol*. It is thought that the Indonesian word for cabbage comes from the Dutch word *kool*. This dish can easily be served as a main course. I call for a range of shrimp paste because it has a strong flavor that one needs to adjust to, so if you have never used it, start with the smaller amount.

1. Preheat a toaster oven to 400°F, Wrap the shrimp paste in aluminum foil and roast for 5 minutes, turning once. Set aside.

2. In a large wok or saucepan, heat the oil over high heat, then cook the curry leaves for 10 seconds. Add the onions, garlic, chiles, and shrimp paste and cook, stirring so that it doesn't stick, until the mixture turns a darker color, about 6 minutes. Add the coconut cream, lemon zest, and salt, stir well, and bring the liquid to a near boil. Add the cabbage, reduce the heat to low, and simmer, uncovered, until the cabbage is cooked but still crisp, about 5 minutes. Stir in the tamarind water and serve.

½ to 1 teaspoon shrimp paste

2 tablespoons peanut oil

3 curry leaves (below)

2 medium-size onions, grated

2 large garlic cloves, very finely chopped

4 fresh red finger-type chiles or 5 fresh red jalapeño chiles, very finely chopped

1½ cups coconut cream (see page 21)

Two 2-inch-long strips lemon zest, white pith removed

1 teaspoon salt

1 pound savoy or green cabbage, cored and shredded

1 tablespoon tamarind paste dissolved in 2 tablespoons hot water

Curry Leaves

Curry leaves have nothing to do with curry. They are the slightly pungent and aromatic leaves of a small tree native to the Himalaya region and are used in Indian cooking. They are usually found in Indian markets, sometimes fresh as well as frozen, and they are sold at some farmers markets, especially in southern California.

Shakhshukha

2 small eggplant (14 to 16 ounces), peeled and sliced into ½-inch-thick rounds

Salt to taste

2 large green bell peppers

1 pound ripe plum tomatoes

1 fresh green finger-type chile or 2 fresh green jalapeño chiles

1 cup extra-virgin olive oil

2 medium-size zucchini (8 to 9 ounces), peeled and sliced into ½-inch-thick rounds

10 large garlic cloves, finely chopped

¼ cup finely chopped fresh parsley leaves

Freshly ground black pepper to taste

1 teaspoon cayenne pepper

4 large eggs, beaten

Makes 6 servings

I've written about *shakhshukha* before and so have many food writers, all describing this Algerian and Tunisian dish as a kind of spicy ratatouille finished with eggs. The ratatouille analogy is fair enough, although I think this dish is more substantial, and it is made in countless different ways. *Shakhshukha* is not an Arabic word, but a Turkish one, and the preparation appears to derive from the nearly identical Turkish dish called *menemen*.

1. Lay the eggplant pieces on some paper towels and sprinkle with salt. Leave them to drain of their bitter juices for 30 minutes.

2. Meanwhile, prepare a hot charcoal fire or preheat a gas grill on high or preheat the oven to 425°F. Place the bell peppers, tomatoes, and chile on the grilling grate or a baking sheet and grill or bake until the skin blisters black all over the peppers and chile and the skins are coming off the tomatoes, 30 to 40 minutes (less time for the chile). Once cool enough to handle, peel the peppers and tomatoes and remove their seeds. Cut the peppers and chiles into strips and the tomatoes into rounds.

3. Pat the eggplant dry with paper towels. Cut all the eggplant slices in half. In a large casserole, heat the olive oil over medium-high heat, then add the eggplant and cook, turning only once, until light golden, about 4 minutes. Remove the eggplant with a slotted ladle and set aside to drain. Turn off the heat and let the oil cool significantly, about 20 minutes.

4. Turn the heat to low, then add the roasted peppers, tomatoes, and chile, along with the zucchini, garlic, and parsley to the casserole. Season with salt, black pepper, and cayenne pepper, cover, and simmer until most of the liquid is evaporated, about 30 minutes. Add the eggplant.

5. Season the eggs with a little salt and black pepper and whisk in a few tablespoons of the broth from the casserole. Make a well in the center of the casserole, raise the heat to high for a minute, then stir the eggs into the well and let them set for a minute. Cook, scrambling the eggs until they are congealed, about 6 minutes, folding, not stirring. Serve hot.

Vegetable Kurma

Makes 4 servings

This is a dish from Lucknow, in the Indian state of Uttar Pradesh, that I adapted from the recipe by Sanjay Kumar and Nivedita Srivastava. A *kurma* is a traditional Mogul preparation, a style of cooking derived from the great Muslim empire of India that was founded in 1526 by Baba, who claimed descent from the Mongol conqueror Genghis Khan. It is a thick, spicy, rich brown curry, filled with wonderful flavors from vegetables, nuts, and fruit. The gravy is creamy from the yogurt and spicy from the masala. This dish goes great with Lamb Keema (page 52). The white cheese, or paneer, can be replaced with a Mexican queso fresco or a Syrian white cheese available in Middle Eastern markets, or you can use farmer's cheese or drained cottage cheese in a pinch.

1. Place the ginger, garlic, cilantro, and green chiles in a blender with ¼ cup of the water and blend until a smooth paste forms, scraping down the sides of the blender when necessary.

2. In a large skillet, heat the oil over high heat until very hot, then cook the cubes of cheese until golden brown, about 30 seconds. Remove the cheese with a spatula and set aside, discarding any burnt bits. Remove 2 tablespoons of the oil from the skillet and mix it with the ginger-garlic paste. Let the skillet cool off the heat for 3 minutes, then add the ginger-garlic paste to the pan and cook over medium heat for 5 minutes, sprinkling it with the milk.

3. Add the cauliflower, beans, carrots, peas, potatoes, salt, garam masala, turmeric, cumin, and ground red chile. Cook for 2 minutes, stirring, then add the tomato puree and the remaining ½ cup water. Reduce the heat to low and simmer, partially covered, until the vegetables are soft, about 1 hour.

4. Stir in the yogurt, then add the fried cheese, pineapple, cashews, and almonds and cook for 3 minutes, stirring. Serve immediately.

One ½-inch cube fresh ginger, peeled

2 large garlic cloves

Leaves from 6 sprigs cilantro

4 fresh green finger-type chiles or 5 fresh green jalapeño chiles, stemmed

¾ cup water

6 tablespoons vegetable oil

6 ounces paneer (see headnote), cut into 12 cubes

¼ cup whole milk

¾ cup cauliflower florets, broken into small pieces

¾ cup green beans, trimmed and cut into ½-inch pieces

¾ cup diced carrots

¾ cup fresh or frozen peas

¾ cup diced peeled potatoes

Salt to taste

½ teaspoon garam masala (see box, page 155)

½ teaspoon ground turmeric

½ teaspoon ground cumin

½ teaspoon ground red chile

½ cup fresh or canned tomato puree

½ cup whole plain yogurt or Stabilized Yogurt (page 49)

½ cup cubed pineapple

1 tablespoon whole unsalted cashews

1 tablespoon sliced or slivered almonds

Eggplant Curry

3 small eggplant (about 3 pounds), peeled and sliced into ½-inch cubes

1 teaspoon salt, plus extra for sprinkling

10 tablespoons vegetable oil

3 large onions, thinly sliced

6 fresh green or red finger-type chiles or 8 fresh green or red jalapeño chiles, seeded and finely chopped

4 large garlic cloves, finely chopped

1 tablespoon ground coriander

1 teaspoon ground red chile or cayenne pepper

¼ teaspoon ground turmeric

½ cup dried unsweetened shredded coconut

Juice and pulp of 1 small lemon

1 bay leaf

1 teaspoon toasted sesame seeds, crushed

1 cup water

1 teaspoon palm sugar or brown sugar

1 teaspoon black mustard seeds, toasted or pan-fried without oil until they begin to pop

2 tablespoons finely chopped fresh cilantro leaves

Makes 6 servings

This was the first Indian dish that I successfully cooked some fifty years ago. It's a recipe from Tamil Nadu in South India and I've liked it all these years. It is not terribly hard to do. The tastes are very spicy-hot and luscious, and it goes well with Rice Pilaf (opposite).

1. Lay the eggplant pieces on some paper towels and sprinkle with salt. Leave them to drain of their bitter juices for 30 minutes, then pat dry with paper towels.

2. In a large skillet, heat 4 tablespoons of the oil over medium-high heat, then brown half of the eggplant pieces on all sides, about 6 minutes in all. Remove and set aside. Add another 4 tablespoons oil to the skillet, and, once it is heated, cook the remaining eggplant and set aside.

3. In a large casserole or stockpot, heat the remaining 2 tablespoons oil over medium-high heat, then cook the onions, fresh chiles, garlic, coriander, ground red chile, and turmeric, stirring occasionally, until soft, about 5 minutes. Add the coconut and cook another 2 to 3 minutes, stirring. Add the lemon juice and pulp, 1 teaspoon salt, the bay leaf, sesame seeds, and water. Stir, add the reserved eggplant, cover, reduce the heat to low, and simmer until the eggplant is very tender and the sauce is thick, about 1½ hours. Add the sugar and mustard seeds, stir, and cook for 5 minutes. Stir in the cilantro and remove and discard the bay leaf. Serve immediately.

Rice Pilaf

Makes 6 servings

This is the basic rice pilaf recipe that you can use for any recipe calling for pilaf as an accompaniment to spicy food. The best rice to use for pilaf is basmati or patna long-grain rice, which are available in supermarkets as well as ethnic markets. An American long-grain rice is okay to use, too, but not converted rice.

1. In a large, heavy casserole or saucepan with a tight-fitting lid, melt the clarified butter over medium-high heat, then cook the drained rice for 2 to 3 minutes, stirring frequently. Add the 3¼ cups water and the salt, increase the heat to high, and, once it begins to boil, reduce the heat to very low and cover. Do not stir or uncover the rice for 12 minutes.

2. Remove the cover and check whether the rice is cooked and the liquid absorbed by pushing a fork to the bottom of the pot in the middle. If there is still liquid in the pot, cook for another 3 minutes and check again.

3. If the water is absorbed but the rice is still hard, add the boiling water and continue cooking until done. The rice can be served immediately or you can cover the pot with a paper towel, replace the lid, and let sit for 10 minutes. When ready to serve, transfer to a serving platter, season with black pepper if desired, fluff the rice, and serve.

2 tablespoons clarified butter (ghee) or unsalted butter

2 cups long-grain rice, rinsed well in a strainer, drained

3¼ cups water

2 teaspoons salt

½ cup boiling water, if needed

Freshly ground black pepper (optional)

Beans and Greens Stew

Makes 8 servings

Traditionally, this Algerian stew called *al-buqul*, which means "greens," or specifically "legumes," would be cooked longer than I cook it here because it would be made with dried legumes that need lots of cooking. I save time by using canned chickpeas and fava beans. The dried white beans, though, do taste much better than the canned here, and they do have to be cooked until almost tender, about 1½ hours, before adding them to the stew. The kind of canned fava beans you are looking for are the round ones called *bath fava* or *foul medammes*, the transliterated name is most likely to be found on the labels of those sold in Middle Eastern markets and in the international section of supermarkets. Mallow is an important part of this stew, but unfortunately it is sold only in farmers markets, perhaps sold under its Japanese name, *fuyu aoi*, or Chinese name, *yuan ye jin kui*. So either you'll have to rely on the farmer or use something else. As we don't have any leafy vegetable remotely similar to mallow in our supermarkets, I suggest you substitute kale or Swiss chard.

1. Bring a medium saucepan of water to a boil over high heat and cook the white beans until tender, about 1¼ hours. Drain and set aside.

2. Bring a large pot of water to a boil over high heat and cook the mallow until wilted, but floating on top, 10 to 12 minutes. Drain and set aside.

3. In a large casserole, heat the olive oil over medium-high heat, then cook the garlic with the tomato paste–water mixture, the dried chile, cayenne pepper, black pepper, and salt, stirring frequently so the garlic doesn't burn, until the water is nearly evaporated, 6 to 8 minutes. Add the water, chickpeas, cooked fava beans, and the reserved white beans, reduce the heat to medium, and cook until almost tender, about 50 minutes. Add the cardoon, potatoes, fresh fava beans, peas, and olives. Stir and cook until the potatoes are almost tender, 40 to 45 minutes.

4. Add the cilantro and mallow, reduce the heat to low, and simmer until the stew is thick and syrupy, about 15 minutes. Remove and discard the dried chile. Serve hot or cold.

1 cup small dried white beans

3 bunches mallow (about ¾ pound) or ¾ pound Swiss chard or kale, well washed, all stems removed, and chopped coarsely

½ cup extra-virgin olive oil

4 large garlic cloves, thinly sliced

1 tablespoon tomato paste dissolved in ¼ cup water

1 dried chile de árbol

1 tablespoon cayenne pepper

1½ teaspoons freshly ground black pepper

1½ teaspoons salt

2½ cups cold water

1½ cups cooked chickpeas, drained

1½ cups cooked fava beans, drained

1 cardoon stalk, diced and boiled for 1 hour in water with ¼ cup vinegar, or 4 large fresh artichoke hearts, diced, or 3 celery ribs, cut into 1-inch lengths

2 medium-size potatoes (about 10 ounces), peeled and diced

1 cup fresh fava beans (from about 1¼ pounds of pods), skinned

1 cup fresh or frozen peas

½ cup pitted green olives

Leaves from 1 bunch fresh cilantro, finely chopped

Firecrackers

12 large fresh green jalapeño chiles

4 ounces Monterey Jack cheese, cut into 1-inch-long x ¼-inch-thick sticks

6 cups vegetable oil, for frying

All-purpose flour or finely ground blue corn flour, for dredging

2 large eggs, beaten

Salt to taste

Makes 6 servings

In the late 1980s and early 1990s, American chefs were finding inspiration in the cooking of the American Southwest, and lots of hot sauces and chiles were being used in new and interesting ways. I was living in Cambridge, Massachusetts, when a restaurant opened called the Cottonwood Café, with lots of Navaho themes in its decor and invented dishes that I liked. I had a dish similar to this there, although I have no idea who made it up. I remember that their version was rolled in blue corn flour before frying. These appetizers are very popular now, and many restaurants and bars sell them at happy hour. They derive from a Mexican preparation. They are sometimes called poppers.

1. Preheat the oven to 450°F. Arrange the chiles on a baking sheet and roast until the skins become crinkly, about 25 minutes. Remove from the oven and, once they are cool enough to handle, peel and slit the chiles lengthwise with a small paring knife and remove the seeds. Stuff the chiles with the cheese, securing the opening of each chile with a toothpick if necessary.

2. Preheat the oil to 360°F in a deep-fryer or an 8-inch saucepan fitted with a basket insert. Dredge the chiles in the flour, then dip them in the egg, and back in the flour again. Cook the stuffed chiles in batches, without crowding the fryer, until golden, 3 to 4 minutes. Drain, sprinkle with salt, and serve immediately.

Spiced Tofu Squares

Makes 6 servings

This Korean dish, called *tofu jon*, is from my friend Unjoo Lee Byars, who instructs that it is important to have properly drained tofu in order for the preparation to work. Make sure it drains for at least a half hour in a colander, and then pat it dry with paper towels. When you shop for tofu, which is usually sold in plastic tubs, it will be marked for different consistencies, from soft to extra firm. For this dish you want extra-firm tofu.

1. In a small bowl, blend together three-quarters of the scallions, the garlic, soy sauce, red chile, sesame seeds, sesame oil, and sugar. Set the dressing aside.

2. In a large nonstick skillet, heat the vegetable oil over medium heat, then cook the tofu pieces, turning once, until light golden on both sides, about 10 minutes. Spread about 1 teaspoon of the dressing over the top of each piece and cook until it looks melted, about 3 minutes. Remove the tofu from the oil and drain. Sprinkle with the remaining scallions and serve.

2 scallions, white and light green parts only, split lengthwise and chopped

4 large garlic cloves, finely chopped

3 tablespoons soy sauce

2 tablespoons ground Korean red chile or 1½ tablespoons ground red chile

2 tablespoons toasted sesame seeds

2 tablespoons sesame oil

1 tablespoon sugar

3 tablespoons vegetable or canola oil

16 to 18 ounces extra-firm tofu, cut in 2 x ½-inch pieces, drained in a colander for 30 minutes, and patted dry with paper towels

Yam Curry

in Chile Gravy

Makes 6 servings

This dish, from the southernmost Indian state of Tamil Nadu, is called *sennaikkai kootu* in Tamil, which means something like "curry in gravy," and it is fiery, which is typical of most southern Indian cooking. Tamil Nadu is known for its spicy-hot vegetarian fare. The yams used in this old and traditional preparation are Old World yams, not American sweet potatoes, which are sometimes called yams, but they are from an entirely different plant family.

1. Place the pigeon peas in a saucepan with cold water to just barely cover and boil over high heat until tender, about 25 minutes. Drain and set aside. Place the yams in a saucepan with salted water to cover by 1 inch, add the tamarind and turmeric, and boil until tender over high heat, about 25 minutes.

2. While the yams are cooking, place the fresh coconut, chickpea flour, red chiles, and asafoetida, if using, in a food processor and grind completely, scraping down the sides when necessary. When the yams are tender, add the coconut mixture to the pot and cook at a boil for 1 minute.

3. In a small skillet, heat the oil over medium heat, then cook the mustard seeds, black gram, and shredded coconut until the mustard seeds start to jump, about 2 minutes. Add this mixture to the yams along with the cooked pigeon peas. Add the curry leaves, if using, season with salt, and cook on low heat, uncovered, until dense, completely tender, and not so liquidy, 1 to 1¼ hours. Garnish with the cilantro and serve.

1 cup pigeon peas or split green peas

1 pound yams, malanga, ñame, or sweet potatoes, peeled and cut into ½-inch cubes

½ cup tamarind pulp or 1 ounce tamarind paste

½ teaspoon ground turmeric

½ coconut, shelled, peeled, and flesh cut up into chunks, or 1 cup dried unsweetened shredded coconut

1 teaspoon chickpea flour, gram flour, or corn flour

10 fresh red finger-type chiles or 14 fresh red jalapeño chiles, seeded and chopped

Pinch of asafoetida (optional)

1 tablespoon vegetable oil

½ teaspoon black mustard seeds

½ teaspoon black gram (urad dal) or black lentils

1 teaspoon dried unsweetened shredded coconut

6 small curry leaves (see page 123; optional)

Salt to taste

1 cup coarsely chopped fresh cilantro leaves

Pumpkin Stew

with Chiles and Cheese

Makes 6 servings

This pumpkin stew is so rewarding that I think serving it as a main course makes a lot of sense. It's orange and white and soul-warming from the chiles. This dish is popular in Peru and Bolivia. This recipe is adapted from the original source, Felipe Rojas-Lombardi's *South American Cooking*. Serve with a green salad on the side.

In a casserole, heat the oil over medium-high heat, then cook the onion, garlic, and chiles, stirring, until soft, about 5 minutes. Add the pumpkin, potatoes, water, salt, and black pepper. Stir, then cover, reduce the heat to low, and simmer until the pumpkin and potatoes are tender, 40 to 45 minutes. Add the half-and-half and 1 cup of the cheese and cook, stirring gently, until the cheese has melted, about 5 minutes. Season with more salt and black pepper if desired and garnish with the remaining cheese. Serve immediately.

1 tablespoon vegetable or safflower oil

1 medium-size onion, finely chopped

2 large garlic cloves, finely chopped

6 fresh green serrano chiles, finely chopped

2 pounds pumpkin or other winter squash, peeled and cubed

2 medium-size white potatoes, peeled and cubed

1 cup water

2 teaspoons salt, or more to your taste

½ teaspoon freshly ground black pepper, or more to your taste

¼ cup half-and-half

1¼ cups diced Mexican queso blanco or farmer's cheese (about 6 ounces)

Chiles Rellenos

1 pound ripe tomatoes, peeled and seeded

½ small onion, quartered

2 large garlic cloves, chopped

1½ tablespoons pork lard

3 whole cloves

4 whole black peppercorns

1 bay leaf

1 cinnamon stick

⅛ teaspoon dried thyme

2 cups chicken broth (homemade or canned)

4 fresh large poblano chiles (see box, opposite)

1½ cups shredded Monterey Jack and white cheddar cheese, combined

2 cups vegetable oil, for frying

3 large eggs, separated

Salt to taste

Makes 2 to 4 servings

This famous dish, served all over Mexico and in every Mexican restaurant in the United States, is filled with either a picadillo, a ground pork stuffing, or with a cheese stuffing. In this recipe, I stuff poblano chiles with cheese, although you can also use New Mexico (Anaheim) chiles. In Mexico, the typical cheese used would be a queso fresco. I use a combination of Monterey Jack and mild white cheddar, since these are good melting cheeses and are readily available.

1. Put the tomatoes, onion, and garlic in a blender and blend until very smooth. In a large skillet, melt the lard over high heat, then cook the tomato puree until bubbling vigorously, about 3 minutes, stirring constantly. Add the cloves, peppercorns, bay leaf, cinnamon stick, thyme, and chicken broth, bring to a boil, and cook at a boil for 3 minutes. Reduce the heat to medium and cook until it is a slightly dense, smooth sauce, about 25 minutes. Keep hot over low heat while you do the next step.

2. Meanwhile, hold the chiles with tongs over a high flame, or under a broiler, until the skin starts to blister and blacken all over, turning the chiles so they blister evenly, 8 to 10 minutes. Place the chiles in a paper bag for 15 minutes to allow the skin to come off easily. Wash the skin off under running water. Make a slit running three-quarters down one side of each chile and carefully remove the seeds and any thick white veins with a sharp paring knife, making sure that you don't cut all the way through the flesh of the chiles and that the stems remain intact and attached. Pat the chiles dry with paper towels.

3. Divide the cheese evenly into four pieces and molded them with your hands into oval shapes narrow enough to fit into the opening of each pepper. Set aside on a paper towel-lined plate and cover with paper towels to absorb more water. If the chiles are wet, their batter will not adhere to them properly for frying.

4. Preheat the frying oil in a large skillet over medium-high heat for 10 minutes or to 375°F. Prepare the batter by beating the egg whites in a medium-size bowl until they form stiff peaks. Add the salt and the yolks, one at a time, beating each one in before adding the next one. Pat the chiles dry again, making sure the outside of each chile is completely dry, then dredge in the flour, tapping off any excess, and dip into the batter completely. Cook the chiles, in batches if necessary so that the skillet isn't crowded, until golden, about 4 minutes, turning once with tongs. Remove to an ovenproof dish and keep warm in a low oven as you continue cooking the chiles.

5. Transfer a few ladlefuls of sauce to a wide, shallow platter and place the fried chiles in the center so the broth comes up about halfway. Serve immediately.

Poblano, Ancho, and Pasilla Chiles

American supermarkets regularly label poblano chiles as pasilla chiles. Here's what you need to know to buy the right item: a poblano chile, generally, is a dark green–colored heart-shaped chile about the size of a small fist. When a poblano chile is sold in its dried state, it is called an ancho chile. A pasilla chile is a darker green than a poblano and is longer and narrower.

Chapter 7

KNOCK-OUT
Noodles &
Rice

Wicked Spaghetti
with Chipotle Chiles in Adobo and Pine Nut Sauce

One 7-ounce can chipotle chiles
   in adobo, chiles chopped and
   sauce reserved

½ cup dry red wine

1 tablespoon tomato paste

1½ tablespoons pine nuts

Salt to taste

1¼ pounds spaghetti

1 to 2 cups freshly grated
   Pecorino cheese

Makes 6 servings

I invented this recipe long ago, long before I began writing cookbooks. I went through a period in the mid-1980s when I just loved super-hot food and dreamed up all kinds of spicy stuff. I call this wicked spaghetti because it has an extremely hot sauce. You will need very little to flavor a lot of pasta. To fully enjoy the heat, it is best to cut it with something such as a salad or bread afterward.

1. In a saucepan, combine the chipotle chiles and their sauce with the red wine, tomato paste, and pine nuts and cook over medium heat until heated through, about 10 minutes.

2. Meanwhile, bring a large pot of abundantly salted water to a rolling boil, then cook the spaghetti until al dente. Drain without rinsing. Toss the pasta with the sauce and top with lots of Pecorino cheese.

Cayobo's "Devil's Nightmare" Pasta

Makes 6 servings

This recipe is from Cayobo's Reggae Lounge in Key West, Florida, created by a guy nicknamed Cayobo who renovates old conch houses. It's not a traditional recipe but a new invention, Cayobo says, which came about when he was experimenting with pasta and chiles. The bananas and orange cut the heat, but it's still one hell of a hot meal. Having spent much time in the Florida Keys, I can tell you that this dish is typical of wacky Keys cooking by those very distinctive Keys personalities—and really good, too.

1. In a large skillet, heat the oil over medium heat, then cook the onion and bell pepper, stirring, until soft and orange-tinged, about 10 minutes. Add the bananas, chiles, orange juice, and pineapple juice. Cook, stirring gently, until the bananas are soft, about 5 minutes. Remove from the heat and stir in the lime juice, cilantro, and Parmesan cheese.

2. Meanwhile, bring a large pot of abundantly salted water to a rolling boil, then cook the fettuccine until al dente. Drain the pasta without rinsing and toss with the butter. Toss again with the sauce and salt and black pepper to taste, mixing well. Serve immediately.

2 tablespoons extra-virgin olive oil

1 medium-size onion, finely diced

1 red bell pepper, finely diced

2 bananas, peeled and sliced ½ inch thick

4 fresh Scotch bonnet chiles or fresh habanero chiles, finely chopped

Juice of 3 oranges

¼ cup pineapple juice

¼ cup fresh lime juice

¼ cup chopped fresh cilantro leaves

¼ cup freshly grated Parmesan cheese

1 pound fettuccine

2 tablespoons unsalted butter

Salt and freshly ground black pepper to taste

Darlene's Special Pasta

2 pounds fresh large shrimp with their heads or 1 pound headless large shrimp, heads and/or shells removed and reserved

2 cups water

1 tablespoon salt, plus more for the pasta

1½ teaspoons freshly ground black pepper

1½ teaspoons cayenne pepper

½ teaspoon freshly ground white pepper

¼ teaspoon dried oregano

¼ teaspoon garlic powder

¼ teaspoon finely chopped fresh basil

½ cup (1 stick) unsalted butter

½ celery rib, finely chopped

¼ cup finely chopped green bell pepper

¼ cup finely chopped red bell pepper

3 scallions, finely chopped

1 fresh or canned artichoke bottom, finely chopped

3 fresh green serrano chiles, finely chopped

3 tablespoons cognac

½ cup heavy cream

12 shucked raw oysters

1 pound spaghetti

Makes 6 servings

I made up this dish in the early 1980s when I was going through my newly found Cajun phase, which I later discovered was actually a Paul Prudhomme phase. This dish is named after a long-lost friend of mine. I cooked a dinner for the two of us that was to be purposely spicy and hot, and I told her that if it was any good I would name this special dish after her. Well, it was delicious, so here you go.

1. Place the heads and/or shells of the shrimp in a saucepan and cover with the water. Bring to a boil over high heat, then reduce the heat to low and simmer while you continue the preparation.

2. Make the seasoning mix by combining 1 tablespoon salt, the black pepper, cayenne pepper, white pepper, oregano, garlic powder, and basil in a small bowl, tossing all the ingredients together. In a large bowl, sprinkle the shrimp with all of the seasoning mix and set aside.

3. To make the sauce, in a large skillet, melt ¼ cup of the butter over medium-high heat, then cook the celery, green bell pepper, red bell pepper, scallions, artichoke, and serrano chiles, stirring almost constantly, until softened, about 5 minutes. Strain the simmering shrimp broth, pour 1 cup broth into the skillet, and cook, stirring, until it is almost evaporated. Add the cognac and cook for 2 minutes. Add the cream, the reserved shrimp, the oysters, and remaining ¼ cup butter. Cook, stirring often, until the oysters begin to shrivel on the edges, which should be at about the same time the butter finishes melting, about 5 minutes.

4. Meanwhile, bring a large pot of abundantly salted water to a rolling boil, then cook the spaghetti until just al dente. Drain without rinsing. Once the sauce is nice and velvety, add the pasta. Cook, tossing well, for 1 to 2 minutes over high heat. Serve immediately.

Drunkard's Fried Noodles
with Seafood

35 fresh green Thai chiles or 15 fresh green serrano chiles, stemmed and quartered lengthwise

4 lemongrass stalks, tough outer portions removed and finely chopped

8 large garlic cloves, finely chopped

1½ teaspoons salt, or more to your taste

Juice from 3 limes

¼ cup Thai fish sauce

1½ tablespoons tamarind paste dissolved in 3 tablespoons hot water

Salt

¾ pound wide rice noodles (pad Thai)

¼ cup peanut oil

1 pound mixed shrimp, scallops, and squid, cleaned with shells removed

4 shallots, thinly sliced

2 teaspoons freshly ground white pepper, or more to your taste

Makes 4 servings

This Thai dish is called Drunkard's Fried Noodles because the blast of chile is thought to be sobering. A favorite lunch or late-night snack, this spicy stir-fry consists of wide rice noodles, fresh basil, chicken or pork or mixed seafood, seasonings, and a healthy dose of fresh sliced chiles. Tamarind paste can be bought in Indian or Chinese markets or on the Internet.

1. In a mortar, pound the chiles, lemongrass, garlic, and salt until mushy. Set aside. In a small bowl, mix the lime juice, fish sauce, and tamarind water together and set aside.

2. Bring a large saucepan of lightly salted water to a boil and cook the rice noodles until supple, about 3 minutes. Drain and set aside.

3. In a wok, heat the oil over high heat until nearly smoking, then cook the seafood until it turns opaque, about 1 minute. Add the shallots and the chile-garlic mixture and cook for 1 minute. Add the lime juice mixture and cook for 2 minutes. Add the noodles, white pepper, and more salt if desired, and cook until little liquid is left, about 3 minutes. Serve immediately.

Rice Noodles
with Corn and Ginger

Makes 4 servings

I made up this recipe when I became confident enough with my Thai cooking. I learned a lot from friends like Su-Mei Yu, author of *Cracking the Coconut* (Morrow, 2000), by going to Thai Town in Los Angeles, by talking to the street vendors at the Wat Thai temple's weekend food festival in the San Fernando Valley, and by cooking Thai dishes nonstop for months. I was quite proud of myself since this was the first Thai dish I created all by myself.

1. Bring a large saucepan of lightly salted water to a boil and cook the rice noodles until supple, about 3 minutes. Drain and set aside.

2. In a wok, heat the oil over medium-high heat, then cook the corn, shallot, ginger, garlic, mango, tomatoes, chiles, lime juice, and fish sauce until sizzling vigorously and the chiles are soft, about 5 minutes. Add the noodles and toss until well coated, 2 to 3 minutes. Add the cilantro and mint, toss again, and cook for 1 minute. Serve immediately.

Salt

½ pound thin rice noodles

3 tablespoons peanut oil

Kernels from 1 cooked ear of corn

1 large shallot, chopped

One 1-inch cube fresh ginger, peeled and finely chopped

4 large garlic cloves, finely chopped

½ small green mango, peeled and julienned

6 cherry tomatoes, cut in half

15 fresh green Thai chiles or 6 fresh green serrano chiles, chopped

2 tablespoons fresh lime juice

1 tablespoon Thai fish sauce

¼ cup coarsely chopped fresh cilantro leaves

2 tablespoons coarsely chopped fresh mint leaves

Rice Noodles
with Pork and Mint

Makes 4 servings

I became enamored of this dish when I was at the very beginning of researching this project and a good friend recommended a Thai restaurant with an unlikely name in the Westwood section of Los Angeles, an area better known for UCLA students than Thai food, called Mr. Noodle. I ordered this dish, *kwaytiow pad kee mau*, which was a stir-fry of big, flat noodles with pork, tomato, and mint and I thought it very good, plenty hot, and a fine dish to include here. The noodles package is sometimes labeled "extra wide." Everything cooks quickly, so make sure your ingredients are prepared and ready to go.

1. Bring a large pot of salted water to a rolling boil, then cook the noodles according to the package instructions. Drain, rinse in a colander, and set aside in cold water. In a small bowl, mix together 1 tablespoon of the oil, the fish sauce, sugar, soy sauce, the ½ teaspoon salt, and the black pepper and set aside.

2. In a large wok, heat the remaining 3 tablespoons oil over high heat, swirling the wok to coat the sides. Add the garlic and cook, stirring constantly, until golden, about 15 seconds. Add the chiles and cook for another 15 to 30 seconds, stirring. (Remember to keep the vent hood on full to avoid irritation to your eyes, nose, and throat.) Add the pork and stir-fry, breaking up any lumps, until browned, about 2 minutes. Add the fish sauce mixture and cook until the sauce is bubbling, about 1 minute. Drain the noodles and add to the wok. Cook, tossing constantly, until they have absorbed the sauce, about 1 minute. Add the mint and tomatoes and continue cooking and tossing until the mint leaves wilt, about 1 minute. Transfer to a serving platter and garnish with the mint. Serve immediately.

½ teaspoon salt, plus more for the noodles

½ pound ½-inch-wide rice noodles

¼ cup vegetable, canola, or peanut oil

3 tablespoons Thai fish sauce

1 tablespoon palm sugar or light brown sugar

2 teaspoons soy sauce

½ teaspoon freshly ground black pepper

4 large garlic cloves, finely chopped

35 fresh red Thai chiles or 10 fresh red finger-type chiles or 15 fresh red serrano chiles, finely chopped

¼ pound ground pork

¾ cup loosely packed, coarsely chopped fresh mint leaves

6 cherry tomatoes, quartered

1 tablespoon finely chopped fresh mint leaves, for garnish

Ants Climbing a Tree

1 tablespoon soy sauce

1 tablespoon sugar

2 teaspoons Chile Oil (page 69)

2 teaspoons sesame oil

½ pound ground pork

¼ pound bean thread noodles
(2 bunches)

¼ cup peanut oil

8 dried chiles de árbol, seeded
and cut in half

2 teaspoons finely chopped fresh
ginger

4 scallions, white and light green
parts, chopped

1 teaspoon red chile flakes

¼ cup water

Makes 4 servings

Chinese writers and cooks will tell you that the name of this dish comes from the fact that when you hold up the thin noodles with your chopsticks, the bits of meat clinging to them appear like ants climbing a tree. Interestingly, this dish is thought by the Sichuanese to be bland. I include it because, first, it's a wonderful taste, and second, it has enough chiles in it to be considered quite hot by many North Americans. The noodles used in this recipe are made from mung or soy beans and are called bean thread noodles or Oriental vermicelli, cellophane noodles, or glass noodles. They are usually found in the international/Asian section of the supermarket. If you're not normally inclined to use chopsticks, think about it for this dish—it's more fun to eat that way and you can better understand its name.

1. In a medium bowl, stir together the soy sauce, sugar, chile oil, and 1 teaspoon of the sesame oil. Add the ground pork and marinate for 15 to 30 minutes. Soak the noodles in hot water until they are pliable, about 5 minutes. Drain well, then cut them with kitchen scissors into shorter lengths.

2. In a wok, heat the peanut oil over high heat, then cook the chiles and ginger for 15 seconds. Add the pork with the marinade and stir-fry constantly, breaking it up, until it has lost its pinkness, about 1 minute. Add the scallions and chile flakes and stir, and then add the noodles, stirring all the time. Add the water and cook until the liquid has been absorbed and evaporated, about 3 minutes. Sprinkle the remaining 1 teaspoon sesame oil on top and toss. Serve immediately.

Pork Fried Rice

Makes 4 to 6 servings

Although pork fried rice is ubiquitous on Chinese take-out menus, this fried rice dish, called *kao pad moo*, is Thai, and it is one of my favorite fried rice dishes. There are some key things to remember when making fried rice so that it doesn't turn into an unappetizing gloppy mess that looks like a pathetic risotto: cook the rice properly, make sure it is cool or cold and dry, and use plenty of oil.

1. In a wok, heat the oil over high heat, swirling the wok to coat the sides with the oil, and cook the garlic until turning brown, 15 to 30 seconds, stirring constantly. Add the shallots and cilantro roots until sizzling furiously, about 1 minute. Add the pork and stir-fry until it loses color, about 2 minutes.

2. Add the rice, stirring and tossing until the grains are broken up and mixed with the other ingredients, then add the fish sauce and sugar. Stir and toss until mixed well. Push the rice to the sides of the wok, making a well in the middle. Pour the egg into the center and let it set for a minute, then start to scramble the egg with small circular stirring movements. Once it has set, stir the egg into the rice and cook for 1 minute. Add three-quarters of the chiles to the wok and toss until well mixed. Transfer to a serving platter and sprinkle the top with the cucumbers, scallions, cilantro, and remaining chiles. Serve immediately.

3 tablespoons vegetable oil

5 large garlic cloves, finely chopped

3 shallots, thinly sliced

2 tablespoons chopped fresh cilantro roots and/or stems

¼ pound pork tenderloin, very thinly sliced in strips

4 cups cooked cold jasmine rice

3 tablespoons Thai fish sauce

1 tablespoon palm sugar or granulated sugar

1 large egg, beaten

½ cup thinly sliced fresh red chiles, such as Thai chiles, finger-type chiles, or serrano chiles

2 small Persian cucumbers, julienned, or ½ regular cucumber, peeled, seeded, and julienned

2 scallions, thinly sliced on the bias

¼ cup coarsely chopped fresh cilantro leaves

Red Rice
with Crispy-Fried Pork

3 tablespoons lard

1 cup medium-grain rice, soaked in tepid water for 30 minutes or rinsed well in a strainer, drained

1 small onion, finely chopped

1 garlic clove, finely chopped

1 large carrot, peeled and finely diced

½ celery rib, finely chopped

1 ripe juicy large tomato (about 10 ounces), cut in half, seeds squeezed out, and grated against the largest holes of a grater

½ cup fresh or frozen peas

2 fresh green jalapeño chiles, sliced

1 tablespoon finely chopped fresh parsley leaves

1 cup chicken broth (homemade or store-bought)

3 tablespoons fresh lemon juice

1 teaspoon salt

Freshly ground black pepper to taste

1 pound pork loin, cut into ¾-inch cubes

4 sprigs cilantro, for garnish

Makes 4 servings

This famous dish is called, simply enough, *arroz a la Mexicana*, Mexican rice, because it is made everywhere in Mexico. Depending on the region you're in, it will have variations, perhaps with meat or fish. This particular version comes from Oaxaca and is made with pork. It can be eaten as either a side dish or a main course.

1. In a heavy saucepan, melt 2 tablespoons of the lard over medium heat, then cook the rice and onion, stirring frequently, until lightly browned and sticking, about 7 minutes. Add the garlic and cook for 1 minute, stirring.

2. Add the carrot, celery, tomato, peas, chiles, parsley, chicken broth, lemon juice, salt, and black pepper. Bring to a boil, stir, reduce the heat to low, cover, and cook until the liquid is absorbed, about 15 minutes. Remove the rice from the heat, insert paper towels between the pot and the lid, and let sit for 10 minutes.

3. Meanwhile, in a medium skillet, heat the remaining 1 tablespoon lard over medium-high heat and cook the pork until crispy brown, 3 to 4 minutes. Turn and cook the other side until browned, another 3 to 4 minutes. Transfer the rice to a serving platter and fluff it with a fork. Add the fried pork and serve hot, garnished with cilantro.

Coconut Chile Rice

with Pigeon Peas and Tamarind Juice

1 teaspoon salt, plus more for the water

½ cup (about ¼ pound) dried pigeon peas or split green peas

6 fresh red finger-type chiles or 8 fresh red jalapeño chiles

1¼ cups grated fresh coconut or dried unsweetened shredded coconut

1 teaspoon yellow split peas

1 teaspoon black gram (urad dal)

½ teaspoon ground turmeric

¼ teaspoon ground fenugreek

Pinch of asafoetida

2 tablespoons clarified butter (ghee)

1 cup long-grain basmati rice, soaked in tepid water for 30 minutes or rinsed well in a strainer, drained

1¾ cups water

1½ tablespoons tamarind paste dissolved in 3 tablespoons hot water

¼ teaspoon garam masala (see box, opposite)

1 tablespoon vegetable oil

¼ cup (1 ounce) unsalted cashews

4 curry leaves (see page 123)

½ teaspoon black mustard seeds

Makes 6 servings

In the city of Mysore in the Indian state of Karnataka, this is a favorite dish. It is fragrant, hot, and filling. The ingredients list appears exotic and it is—the pigeon peas, fresh coconut, black gram, fenugreek, asafoetida, tamarind, black mustard seeds, and curry leaves can only be found in Indian markets or online. I assure you it's worth the effort.

1. Bring a large saucepan of water to a boil, salt lightly, and cook the pigeon peas until soft, about 20 minutes. Drain and set aside.

2. Preheat the oven to 450°F. Place the chiles in one baking dish or sheet and the coconut, yellow split peas, and black gram in another. Roast until the chiles are slightly blackened and the coconut is browning on the edges, about 25 minutes for the chiles and 10 to 12 minutes for the coconut. When they are cool enough to handle, remove the stems and seeds from the chiles. Transfer the contents of both baking dishes to a food processor, add the turmeric, fenugreek, and asafoetida, and grind to a paste, scraping down the sides if necessary. Set aside.

3. In a large, heavy casserole or saucepan with a tight-fitting lid, melt 1 tablespoon of the clarified butter over medium-high heat and cook the rice for 2 to 3 minutes, stirring frequently. Add the 1¾ cups water, 1 teaspoon salt, the pigeon peas, coconut-chile paste, tamarind water, and garam masala. Increase the heat to high, stir, and, once it begins to boil slightly, reduce the heat to low, cover, and cook without stirring or uncovering until the liquid is absorbed and the rice is tender, 15 to 18 minutes.

4. Meanwhile, in a small skillet, heat the oil over medium-high heat, then cook the cashews, curry leaves, and mustard seeds until the mustard seeds start to crackle and pop, 1 to 2 minutes. Transfer the rice to a serving platter, fluff the rice, and pour the mustard seed mixture over the top. Drizzle the remaining 1 tablespoon of melted clarified butter over the top. Serve immediately.

Indian Spice Blends

There are three spice blends used predominantly in Indian cooking. These are curry powder, which is sold everywhere, garam masala, and *panch phoron*. The most prominent spice in curry powder is coriander seed. It also contains turmeric, which is what makes the spice look golden, and lesser amounts of cumin, fenugreek, fennel, yellow mustard seeds, cloves, white pepper, and very little red chile pepper. Garam masala is used mostly in northern India, especially in Mogul cuisine, but can be found in South Africa used in Cape Malay cooking. Although it is found premade in jars in many Indian markets and large supermarkets, it can be made at home by blending together equal amounts of ground cumin, coriander, cardamom, and black pepper, and then adding a much lesser amount of cloves, nutmeg, cinnamon, and saffron. It's usually a rust color. *Panch phoron* (see box on page 162) is a spice mix typical in Bengali cuisine. It is a blend of equal amounts of ground cumin, fennel, and black mustard with a little lesser amount of nigella and fenugreek. This spice mix is usually sold premixed but unground in Indian markets.

Shrimp and Chile Fried Rice

Makes 4 to 6 servings

Fried rice is tricky to make. You start with steamed rice and make sure it is cool or cold and not warm. Fried rice requires a good bit of oil in order for the grains to remain separate and to make sure the final dish doesn't end up looking like risotto. Another thing you want to remember is that the eggs should begin to congeal before you start stirring them. So it's best to leave the eggs undisturbed for a bit until the white starts turning opaque. Then you can scramble them a bit, but not too much. You want the rice to be yellow from the yolk but you want to avoid making the rice creamy. Wait for the egg to cook before you add the next ingredient. Most Thai rice dishes are mild, one reason why they are popular with tourists, but this dish is quite hot.

1. In a wok, heat the oil over medium-high heat and cook the shallots and chiles until the shallots are soft, about 5 minutes. Add the red curry paste and cook, stirring, until blended into the shallots and the oil starts to separate, 3 to 4 minutes.

2. Add the pork tenderloin and pork belly and cook for 2 minutes, stirring. Add the cold rice and stir and toss thoroughly with a spoon or paddle until the rice is colored with the curry paste and heated through, 5 to 6 minutes. Raise the heat to high and push the rice to the sides, to make a well in the center of the wok. Pour the eggs into the well, let them set slightly, and then start to scramble the eggs with a small circular stirring movement. Once they are fully cooked, about 2 minutes, stir in the shrimp. Stir in the fish sauce, cook for 1 minute, then remove from the heat and transfer to a platter. Sprinkle with the scallions and cilantro and decorate the borders with the red chiles. Serve immediately.

¾ cup peanut oil

3 large shallots, finely chopped

20 fresh green Thai chiles or 8 fresh green serrano chiles, finely chopped

1 tablespoon Red Curry Paste (page 22)

⅔ cup diced uncooked pork tenderloin or ham

⅓ cup diced or sliced raw pork belly or blanched bacon

4 cups cooked cold jasmine rice

3 large eggs, beaten lightly

1 cup cooked small shrimp

3 tablespoons Thai fish sauce

4 scallions, finely chopped, for garnish

2 tablespoons finely chopped fresh cilantro leaves, for garnish

4 fresh serrano chiles, split into quarters with a paring knife but keeping the chile whole and attached to the stem end, for garnish

Pasta Balls
with Merguez Sausages

6 tablespoons extra-virgin olive oil

1 ounce mutton or lamb fat, chopped

1 medium-size onion, finely chopped

1 piece plain beef or lamb jerky (about 2 ounces), chopped

¾ pound merguez sausages, casings removed and crumbled

2 large ripe tomatoes (about 1 pound), peeled, seeded, and chopped

2 tablespoons tomato paste dissolved in ¼ cup water

2 tablespoons Harissa (page 25)

1 teaspoon Tabil (opposite)

1 tablespoon freshly ground black pepper

1 tablespoon cayenne pepper

4 cups fresh fava beans (from about 5 pounds of pods), skinned

2 cups fresh or frozen peas

2 cups water

Salt to taste

1 pound toasted pasta balls (see headnote)

2 fresh finger-type chiles or 4 fresh red jalapeño chiles, seeded and finely chopped

5 dried organic rosebuds, crumbled (optional)

Makes 8 servings

Muhammas is the Tunisian Arabic name for what Middle Eastern groceries sell as *moghrabiye*, dried and toasted pasta balls that are the size of coriander seeds. They are also sold as "toasted pasta balls" and as "Israeli couscous." This richly flavored and hot springtime dish uses merguez sausages (*mirqaz* in Tunisian Arabic), which are absolutely delicious, highly spiced Tunisian lamb or beef sausages that I used to order everywhere when I was in Tunisia but which were all but unavailable in this country years ago. Today a number of excellent merguez sausages are available, and the ones I use are made by Fabrique Délice or d'Artagnan, both available through the Internet. I call for mutton or lamb fat in this recipe and that's easily enough found—just ask the butcher or, if they make you buy something, get the fattiest cut of lamb, such as shoulder chop, and cut off some of the fat and reserve the meat for another purpose.

1. In a large casserole, heat the olive oil with the mutton fat over medium-high heat until the fat has been sizzling for 1 minute, then cook the onion, stirring, until it is soft, 4 to 5 minutes. Add the jerky, sausages, tomatoes, diluted tomato paste, harissa, tabil, black pepper, and cayenne pepper. Stir then cook for 1 minute. Add the fava beans and peas, add the water, and bring to a boil. Reduce the heat to low and simmer, uncovered, for 30 minutes. Cover and simmer, stirring occasionally, until the vegetables are tender, another 15 minutes.

2. Meanwhile, bring 2 quarts of lightly salted water to a rolling boil, then cook the pasta balls, uncovered, until soft and the water is nearly evaporated, about 15 minutes. Taste the sauce and add salt if desired, then add the sauce to the pasta, stir to mix well, and cook over low heat for about 5 minutes. Transfer to a serving bowl and sprinkle the chopped fresh chiles and rosebuds on top, if using. Serve immediately.

Tabil

Makes about ¼ cup

Tabil, pronounced "table," means "seasoning" in Tunisian Arabic, although it also is the word for coriander. This is an important spice mix in all of Tunisian cooking and it varies from region to region, with some cooks adding dried powdered geranium or rose petals to the blend.

Place all the ingredients in a spice mill and grind until powdery and homogeneous. Alternatively, place in a mortar and pound. Store in a jar and keep with your other spices.

¼ cup coriander seeds

1 tablespoon caraway seeds

2 teaspoons cayenne pepper

2 teaspoons garlic powder

Chapter 8

SIDE OF

Heat

Rice and Peas

1 cup (about ½ pound) dried red kidney beans, soaked overnight in water to cover and drained

½ small coconut, shelled, peeled, and grated, or 1¼ cups dried unsweetened shredded coconut

1 small onion, finely chopped

2 scallions, finely chopped

1 fresh Scotch bonnet chile or fresh habanero chile, finely chopped

1 tablespoon unsalted butter

1 tablespoon salt

1 large garlic clove, finely chopped

2 sprigs fresh thyme

1 teaspoon freshly ground black pepper

½ teaspoon ground allspice

2½ cups medium-grain rice, soaked in tepid water for 30 minutes or rinsed well in a strainer, drained

Makes 8 servings

Jamaican "rice and peas" is a great example of a peasant-based pan-Caribbean type of dish. The combination of rice and beans—and in Jamaica the "peas" are actually red kidney beans or pigeon peas—is a typical dish on Sundays in Jamaica and is often served with meats. While there are regional variations around the Caribbean, Jamaica's is a notably fiery dish. Some cooks don't use the Scotch bonnet chiles in order to make the dish balance with spicier main courses.

1. Place the beans in a large pot with the coconut and cover by 2 inches with cold water. Bring to a boil and boil until tender, about 1½ hours.

2. Add the onion, scallions, fresh chile, butter, salt, garlic, thyme, black pepper, and allspice, reduce the heat to medium-low, and simmer for 15 minutes. Reduce the heat to low, add the rice, and cook until it is tender, about 15 minutes. If the rice is still a little hard, add another cup of boiling water, cover again, and cook until tender. Serve immediately.

Red Lentil Dal

Makes 4 servings

This Bengali-style dal called *masoor dal* is always made with red lentils because they disintegrate well, which is what you want to have happen to have a soft dal.

1. Add the water and the lentils to a large saucepan and bring to a boil. Cook until most of the liquid has evaporated and the lentils are soft, about 12 minutes. Drain through a strainer and mash the lentils.

2. In a large skillet, heat the oil over medium-high heat and cook the cumin seeds and panch phoron for 1 minute. Add the onion and cook, stirring, until golden brown, 6 to 8 minutes. Add the mashed lentils, chile, salt, and turmeric, reduce the heat to low, and simmer until dense and about the consistency of a bowl of oatmeal, about 15 minutes. Serve hot.

3 cups water

1 cup red lentils

1 tablespoon vegetable oil

½ teaspoon cumin seeds

½ teaspoon panch phoron (see box)

1 medium-size onion, sliced

1 fresh green finger-type chile or 2 fresh green jalapeño chiles, seeded and finely chopped

½ teaspoons salt

½ teaspoon ground turmeric

Panch Phoron

Panch phoron is a spice mixture unique to Bengal. It consists of equal parts whole onion seeds, celery seeds, anise seeds, fenugreek, cumin, nigella, and *radhuni*; mustard seeds can replace *radhuni*. *Panch phoron* is sold as a premixed spice in Indian markets. If you like, you can add ½ teaspoon to every Bengal dish that you make. *Panch phoron* is also available via the Internet.

Zucchini
with Tomatoes, Corn, and Chiles

Makes 4 servings

This delightful dish can be made hotter if you like using more chiles. It will also be a little nicer with fresh corn kernels rather than frozen. You could also cut up some other cooked vegetables (pumpkin is especially nice) and heat them with this dish in the same saucepan.

1. In a large skillet, heat the olive oil over high heat and, when it is almost smoking, cook the zucchini, preferably in one layer, until light brown on both sides, about 6 minutes. Remove the zucchini with a slotted spoon or spatula and set aside.

2. Add the onion and garlic to the skillet and cook, stirring constantly, until soft and light brown, about 3 minutes. Reduce the heat to low, add the bell pepper and chiles, season with salt and black pepper, cover, and simmer until soft, about 10 minutes. Stir in the tomatoes, corn, and cilantro and continue cooking, covered, until the corn is almost tender, 20 to 25 minutes. Add the zucchini and cook until the vegetables are soft, about 10 minutes. Serve immediately.

2 tablespoons extra-virgin olive oil

1 pound small zucchini, sliced ¼ inch thick

1 medium-size onion, thinly sliced

2 large garlic cloves, finely chopped

1 green bell pepper, roasted, peeled and cut into strips

2 fresh green finger-type chiles or 3 fresh green jalapeño chiles, seeded and cut into strips

Salt and freshly ground black pepper to taste

1 pound tomatoes, cut in half, seeds squeezed out, and grated against the largest holes of a grater

1 cup fresh corn kernels

3 tablespoons finely chopped fresh cilantro leaves

Spinach and Pigeon Pea Curry

1 cup pigeon peas or split green peas, rinsed

Salt to taste

1 cup water

1½ pounds spinach, heavy stems removed and chopped

5 tablespoons vegetable oil

6 fresh red finger-type chiles or 8 fresh red jalapeño chiles, seeded and split lengthwise

1 tablespoon coriander seeds

2 cups dried unsweetened shredded coconut

One 1-inch cube tamarind paste

1 teaspoon ground turmeric

2 medium-size onions, chopped

Makes 6 servings

This dish from the southern Indian state of Karnataka is called *soppu palya*. It is a typical side dish preparation from North Karnataka, where it is usually eaten with a variety of rotis (griddled unleavened breads) made from wheat or millet. The final dish should look mushy and creamy.

1. Put the pigeon peas in a medium saucepan, cover with cold water by 3 inches, and bring to a boil over high heat. Salt lightly and cook, stirring once or twice, until the peas are al dente, 10 to 12 minutes. Be careful that you don't cook too long or the peas will disintegrate and become mush. Drain, reserving 1 cup of the cooking water, and return the peas to the saucepan.

2. In another medium saucepan, bring the 1 cup water (not the reserved water) to a boil over high heat, then cook the spinach until soft, about 5 minutes. Transfer the spinach and the liquid it cooked in to the saucepan with the pigeon peas and stir it in.

3. In a medium skillet, heat 1 tablespoon of the oil over medium-high heat, then cook the chiles and coriander seeds, stirring, until the seeds are slightly browned and the skin of the chiles is crinkly, about 4 minutes. Place this mixture in a food processor with the coconut and tamarind paste and grind to a paste. Add this paste to the pigeon pea mixture along with the turmeric. Season with salt and mix well.

4. In the skillet you used to cook the chiles, add the remaining 4 tablespoons oil and heat over high heat, then cook the onions, stirring occasionally, until golden and starting to get crispy, about 6 minutes.

5. Add the cooked onions to the pigeon pea mixture with the reserved 1 cup cooking liquid and cook over medium heat until it comes to a boil. If the mixture looks too dry and it is difficult to stir, add more water, up to 1 cup. Serve hot.

Cabbage Curry

Makes 4 servings

This dish from the Indian state of Kerala is very simple to make, but you want to be sure you don't cook the cabbage too much. It should not be as soft as the onion, but almost.

1. In a large skillet, heat the oil over medium heat, then cook the mustard seeds until they start to crackle and pop, 1 to 2 minutes. Add the onions, chiles, and curry leaves and cook, stirring, until the onions are golden and soft, about 20 minutes.

2. Add the cabbage and salt, toss well to mix, cover, reduce the heat to low, and cook, stirring occasionally, until the cabbage is soft and wilted with only the tiniest of bite to it, about 12 minutes. Add the coconut and cook until fragrant, about 3 minutes. Serve hot.

¼ cup vegetable oil or mustard oil

1 teaspoon black mustard seeds

3 medium-size onions, thinly sliced

4 fresh green finger-type chiles or 8 fresh green serrano chiles, chopped

5 curry leaves (see page 123)

1 small head green cabbage, cored, outer leaves removed, and shredded

2 to 3 teaspoons salt, or more to your taste

2 tablespoons dried unsweetened shredded coconut

Skillet-Fried Potatoes
with Green Chiles

1½ pounds small waxy potatoes, such as Red Bliss

2 tablespoons lard

1 medium-size onion, finely chopped

2 fresh green finger-type chiles or 3 fresh green jalapeño chiles, seeded and cut into strips

Salt to taste

Makes 4 servings

This Mexican preparation is called *papas con rajas*, potatoes with strips—"strips" being slices of chiles. This is a particularly nice accompaniment to Mahimahi with Green Chile and Cilantro Cream Sauce (page 116).

1. Place the potatoes in a saucepan and cover with cold water, then turn the heat to high and cook for 20 minutes. Turn the heat off, let the potatoes rest in the water for 5 minutes, then drain and, when cool enough to handle, peel and cut into ¼-inch-thick slices.

2. In a large skillet, melt the lard over medium heat, then cook the onion and chiles, stirring, until soft, about 5 minutes. Raise the heat to high, add the potatoes and salt, and cook, tossing and turning almost constantly, until golden, about 10 minutes. Serve hot.

Eggplant Bharta

2 medium-size eggplant
(about 2½ pounds)

Salt to taste

3 tablespoons vegetable oil or
mustard oil

1 medium-size onion, finely
chopped

¼ cup finely chopped fresh
cilantro leaves

2 fresh green finger-type chiles
or 3 fresh green jalapeño chiles,
seeded and finely chopped

2 large garlic cloves, crushed
until mushy

1 teaspoon ground cumin

¼ teaspoon ground turmeric

½ cup plain yogurt

Makes 4 to 6 servings

A *bharta* is a class of dishes usually made by boiling or roasting a
vegetable, then mashing it together with a variety of seasonings, but
usually some combination of onions, garlic, and fresh green chiles or dried
red chiles. Ginger and tomatoes are sometimes added as well. This is a
Bengali dish, very nice to eat with some naan.

1. Preheat the oven to 425°F. Cut the eggplants in half, place in a baking dish,
and roast until the skin is crispy, about 35 minutes. Remove the eggplant
from the oven and, once it has cooled, remove the flesh and mash it in a
colander. Season with salt and let it drain for 30 minutes.

2. In a large skillet, heat the oil over medium heat, then cook the onion,
stirring, until golden, 8 to 10 minutes. Add the cilantro, chiles, garlic, cumin,
turmeric, and salt to taste and cook for a few minutes. Add the eggplant and
continue cooking until the eggplant mixture is rather dense and dry, 15 to 20
minutes. Stir in the yogurt and remove from the heat. Serve hot.

Mustard Greens and Chiles

Makes 4 to 6 servings

This dish, called *sarson ki saag*, is from the Punjab. Serve with roti and Lamb Keema (page 52) or Lamb in Spicy Cardamom and Rose Water–Flavored Yogurt Sauce (page 49). The gram flour is found in Indian markets, but you can also use chickpea flour or fine corn flour.

1. Bring a large saucepan filled with the water to a boil over high heat. Add the mustard greens and spinach and cook until soft, about 5 minutes. Drain well through a strainer, pressing out excess liquid with the back of a wooden spoon, or let it sit to drain for 45 minutes.

2. In a large skillet, melt the clarified butter over medium heat, then add the ginger, garlic, green chiles, and red chiles and cook, stirring, until light brown, 3 to 4 minutes. Add the reserved greens and salt. In a small bowl, mix the gram flour with a little water, 2 to 3 tablespoons, and stir into the greens. Reduce the heat to low and simmer until the liquid is mostly evaporated and the greens look mushy, about 30 minutes. Serve hot, with the butter on top.

2 cups water

2 pounds mustard greens, heavy stems removed and finely chopped

½ pound spinach, heavy stems removed and finely chopped

¼ cup clarified butter (ghee)

One 1-inch cube fresh ginger, peeled and very finely chopped

4 large garlic cloves, very finely chopped

2 fresh green finger-type chiles or 3 fresh green jalapeño chiles, seeded and very finely chopped

2 dried chiles de árbol, seeded and crumbled

Salt to taste

2 tablespoons gram flour, chickpea flour, or fine corn flour, sifted

1 tablespoon unsalted butter

Baby Carrots
in the "Sauce That Dances"

Makes 6 servings

In Algeria, this dish can be served as a meze. The title implies that the sauce will be highly seasoned and piquant and dance in your mouth from the chile burn. The Algerian Arabic name also implies that the cook would probably use wild carrots to make it. In fact, this is a good recipe to use to experiment with varieties of carrots such as purple carrots or white carrots that you might encounter at the farmers market. Remember when buying supermarket carrots that those so-called "baby" carrots in a bag are not young carrots at all; they are mature carrots that have been pared down to that shape.

1. Bring a saucepan filled with lightly salted water to a boil and cook the carrots until almost tender, about 5 minutes. Drain and set aside.

2. In a large casserole or skillet over medium-high heat, add the olive oil, tomato paste, water, garlic, dried chiles, caraway, ground chile, salt, and black pepper. Once the mixture begins to boil, reduce the heat to low, cover, and simmer for 10 minutes. Add the carrots and cook until completely tender, about 15 minutes. Add the vinegar, increase the heat to high, and cook for 2 minutes. Serve hot.

¼ cup extra-virgin olive oil

2 tablespoons tomato paste

1 cup water

1 head garlic, peeled as much as possible without separating the cloves

2 dried chiles de árbol

1 teaspoon ground caraway

1 teaspoon ground red chile or cayenne pepper

Salt and freshly ground black pepper to taste

1 tablespoon white wine vinegar

2 pounds young carrots, peeled and trimmed

Fried Plantains
in Chile and Red Palm Oil Sauce

1 cup red palm oil or 1 cup walnut
  oil mixed with 2 teaspoons
  hot paprika

Salt to taste

3 ripe plantains, peeled and sliced
  ½ inch thick

1 medium-size onion, chopped

2 large ripe tomatoes (about 1
  pound), peeled, seeded, and
  chopped

3 fresh cherry chiles or 8 fresh
  red finger-type chiles or 2
  fresh habanero chiles, chopped

1 tablespoon white vinegar
  (optional)

Makes 4 to 6 servings

In small roadside restaurants in the Ivory Coast this dish, *aloco*, is very popular. The plantains are fried in a pan of hot palm oil and seasoned with tomatoes, onions, and chiles, and usually served with grilled fish. Red palm oil is available at African and Caribbean markets or online, and it is the ingredient that will make West African recipes taste West African. Try to find it, but if that proves impossible you can use walnut or peanut oil, although they lack the authentic flavor and color of the palm oil. The plantains required for this preparation must be ripe, meaning that their skins will nearly be black. This means you will have to buy the unripe plantains from the supermarket at least a week before you want to make this dish.

1. In a large skillet, heat the oil over medium-high heat until nearly smoking. Salt the plantains and fry in 2 or 3 batches until golden brown on both sides, 4 to 5 minutes in all. Remove from the oil and drain on paper towels.

2. Add the onion, tomatoes, and chiles to the skillet with the oil that you cooked the plantains in and bring to a gentle boil, then reduce the heat to low and simmer, stirring frequently, until the sauce is thick and chunky, about 45 minutes. Stir in the vinegar if using. Arrange the plantains on a serving platter and pour the sauce over them. Serve immediately.

Spinach with Coconut

⅔ cup dried unsweetened shredded coconut or grated fresh coconut

8 fresh green Thai chiles or 2 large fresh green jalapeño chiles

1 teaspoon salt

½ teaspoon ground cumin

½ teaspoon cayenne pepper

½ teaspoon ground turmeric

2 tablespoons vegetable oil

1 teaspoon black mustard seeds

1 small onion, finely chopped

6 dried Dundicutt chiles or 2 dried chiles de árbol, crumbled

10 curry leaves (optional; see page 123)

2½ pounds spinach, heavy stems removed

Makes 4 servings

This dish from Kerala is known as a *thoren*, a kind of stir-fry dish that can be made with any number of shredded vegetables. It is made with shredded coconut cooked in oil seasoned with mustard seeds, dried red chiles, and fresh curry leaves. The Dundicutt chiles that are typically used in Indo-Pakistani cooking can be ordered from www.penzeys.com (see page 9). The chiles de árbol are the regular whole dried red chile found in the supermarket.

1. In a blender, combine the coconut, green chiles, salt, cumin, cayenne pepper, and turmeric with enough water to make the blades spin, about ½ cup. Run until smooth.

2. In a wok or large skillet, heat the oil over medium-high heat, then cook the mustard seeds until they start to crackle and pop, about 1 minute. Add the onion, dried chiles, and curry leaves, if using, and cook until the onion starts to soften, about 2 minutes. Add the spinach and cook, stirring constantly, until it starts to wilt, about 5 minutes. Stir in the coconut mixture and continue cooking until the spinach is tender, about 5 minutes. Serve hot.

Chile con Queso

Makes 6 servings

This dish from Chihuahua and Sonora in Mexico is nothing but "chiles and cheese," but what a combination! The first time I had something like it was in a Oaxacan restaurant in Los Angeles. What makes it so appealing is that the blistering hot chiles are moderated by the bland cheeses, making for a delightful appetizer. The cheeses used are *queso Chihuahua* and *queso asadero*, both of which can be purchased in many supermarkets in the United States. You can replace them with a mixture of mild white cheddar and white Jack cheeses. The process of blistering the jalapeño chiles might seem like a lot of work, but the way I do it makes it rather simple. I take the flat rack out of my roasting pan and arrange the chiles on it, and then place the rack over the stove burner until the bottom sides of the chiles are completely blackened. Then I turn them over with tongs and do the other side. If you can grill the chiles, all the better; it will be an even better taste.

1. Place the chiles on a flat rack and then place the rack over a burner and turn the heat on to high. Blister the chiles black on all sides, moving the rack and turning the chiles when necessary. Alternatively, you can grill the chiles. Remove the chiles and, when cool enough to handle, rub off as much blackened skin as you can. Cut in half and remove the stem and seeds, then slice into thin strips and set aside.

2. In a medium skillet, heat the oil over medium heat, then cook the onion, stirring, until it is translucent, about 7 minutes. Add the chile strips and tomato to the skillet, cover, and cook, stirring occasionally, until soft, about 8 minutes. Add the cream and cook another 2 minutes. Stir in the cheese until it melts. Season with salt and serve.

30 fresh green jalapeño chiles

¼ cup vegetable oil

1 medium-size onion, thinly sliced

1 ripe medium-size tomato, peeled, seeded, and coarsely chopped

¾ cup light cream

½ pound mixed Mexican queso Chihuahua and queso asadero or mixed mild white cheddar and Monterey Jack cheese, diced

Salt to taste

Chiles and Onions
with Boiled Cheese

Makes 4 servings

This recipe, called *ema datshi,* comes from a Bhutanese native, Kunzang Namgyel, who says that if you've been to Bhutan and not eaten this, you have not been to Bhutan. The Bhutanese like their food hot, and chiles are widespread. How chiles got to Bhutan is a good question, and no one has ever written about it. I believe they arrived in Bhutan from Goa. The only other alternative is that chiles came from Sichuan over the Himalayas. Eat raw chiles dipped in salt to accompany this dish if you like to be authentic. The cheese used in this dish cannot be found outside Bhutan. It is a local cheese made by farmers that doesn't dissolve when put in boiling water. The best substitute is Syrian white cheese, available in Middle Eastern markets, or a Mexican queso fresco, available in Latin American markets and many supermarkets. Serve with steamed rice and a main course.

Put the chiles, onion, and vegetable oil in a medium saucepan and pour in the water. Bring to a boil, then reduce the heat to medium and cook for 8 minutes. Add the tomatoes and garlic and boil for another 2 minutes. Add the cheese and cook for 3 minutes until melted. Add the cilantro, turn off the heat, stir, cover, and let sit for 2 minutes. Serve hot.

½ pound fresh green jalapeño chiles, seeded and quartered lengthwise

1 medium-size onion, chopped

1 tablespoon vegetable oil

1¾ cups water

1 pound tomatoes, peeled, seeded, and chopped

5 large garlic cloves, smashed

½ pound firm Syrian white cheese or Mexican queso fresco, diced

1 tablespoon finely chopped fresh cilantro leaves

Measurement Equivalents

Please note that all conversions are approximate.

LIQUID CONVERSIONS

U.S.	Metric
1 tsp	5 ml
1 tbs	15 ml
2 tbs	30 ml
3 tbs	45 ml
¼ cup	60 ml
⅓ cup	75 ml
⅓ cup + 1 tbs	90 ml
⅓ cup + 2 tbs	100 ml
½ cup	120 ml
⅔ cup	150 ml
¾ cup	180 ml
¾ cup + 2 tbs	200 ml
1 cup	240 ml
1 cup + 2 tbs	275 ml
1¼ cups	300 ml
1⅓ cups	325 ml
1½ cups	350 ml
1⅔ cups	375 ml
1¾ cups	400 ml
1¾ cups + 2 tbs	450 ml
2 cups (1 pint)	475 ml
2½ cups	600 ml
3 cups	720 ml
4 cups (1 quart)	945 ml
	(1,000 ml is 1 liter)

WEIGHT CONVERSIONS

U.S./U.K.	Metric
½ oz	14 g
1 oz	28 g
1½ oz	43 g
2 oz	57 g
2½ oz	71 g
3 oz	85 g
3½ oz	100 g
4 oz	113 g
5 oz	142 g
6 oz	170 g
7 oz	200 g
8 oz	227 g
9 oz	255 g
10 oz	284 g
11 oz	312 g
12 oz	340 g
13 oz	368 g
14 oz	400 g
15 oz	425 g
1 lb	454 g

OVEN TEMPERATURE CONVERSIONS

°F	Gas Mark	°C
250	½	120
275	1	140
300	2	150
325	3	165
350	4	180
375	5	190
400	6	200
425	7	220
450	8	230
475	9	240
500	10	260
550	Broil	290

Sources

Online Shopping

These days you can find practically anything with a Google search online. I've attempted to provide here as many reliable online sources as possible for the specialized foods used in this book. Here are more general websites and a list of where to find specific chiles used in the recipes.

General Websites

www.myspicer.com
An excellent source for spices of all kinds and especially hard-to-find South American chiles

www.penderys.com
A source for a large variety of dried chiles and hot sauces

www.penzeys.com
An excellent source for dried chiles and spices

www.mexgrocer.com
For all your Mexican cooking needs, from chiles to tortillas

www.friedas.com
A great source for specialty fruits and vegetables

www.jbafricanmarket.com
A variety of African food products, including red palm oil

www.gourmetsleuth.com
Food products for Asian, Mexican, and Indian cuisines

www.templeofthai.com
Online Thai market for all items, including sambals for Indonesian cooking

www.asianfoodgrocer.com
Noodles, rice, and other Asian products

www.kingarthurflour.com
Excellent source for flours, unsweetened coconut, and potato starch

www.thaifoodandtravel.com
This excellent site provides a searchable database of Thai markets in the U.S. by ZIP code. Also excellent for Chinese and Indo-Malaysian shopping needs.

Where to Find Specific Chiles

African bird chile, ground
www.herbco.com

ají amarillo chiles, whole or ground
www.myspicer.com
www.penderys.com

ají panca chiles
www.tjpmd.com
www.penderys.com

ancho chiles
www.myspicer.com
www.friedas.com

bird's eye (bird) chiles, whole dried
www.friedas.com

cascabel chiles
www.friedas.com
www.penderys.com

cherry chiles, fresh
www.friedas.com

chiles de árbol, dried
www.myspicer.com
www.friedas.com
www.penzeys.com

chipotle chiles
www.penderys.com

Dundicutt chiles
www.penzeys.com

finger-type chiles, fresh
www.friedas.com

guajillo chiles, dried
www.myspicer.com
www.friedas.com

habanero chiles
www.friedas.com

jalapeño chiles, fresh red and green
www.friedas.com

New Mexico (Anaheim) chiles
www.friedas.com

pasilla chiles, dried
www.myspicer.com

piquín chiles
www.penzeys.com
www.friedas.com
www.penderys.com

piri-piri chiles
www.spicewallabrand.com

poblano chiles
www.friedas.com

rocoto chiles
www.tjpmd.com
www.penderys.com

serrano chiles, fresh red and green
www.friedas.com

Thai chiles, fresh red and green
www.friedas.com

yellow banana chiles, fresh
www.friedas.com

yellow chiles (yellow Caribe), fresh
www.friedas.com
www.friedas.com

Index

Note: Page numbers in italics indicate photos or photo captions.

About the Author

Clifford A. Wright is a cook, cookbook author, and independent culinary historian who won the James Beard Cookbook of the Year award and the Beard award for the Best Writing on Food for *A Mediterranean Feast* in 2000. He is the author of sixteen books, fourteen of which are culinary histories and cookbooks. He is also the author of both popular and scholarly articles on chiles.